THE BIG LEBOWSKI

Ethan Coen
&
Joel Coen

ff

faber and faber

First published in 1998
by Faber and Faber Limited
3 Queen Square London WCIN 3AU

Phototypeset by Intype London Ltd
Printed in England by Clays Ltd, St Ives plc

© Ethan Coen & Joel Coen, 1998

Photographs © Gramercy Pictures, 1998

Ethan Coen and Joel Coen are hereby identified as authors of this
work in accordance with Section 77 of the Copyright,
Designs and Patents Act 1988

A CIP record for this book
is available from the British Library

ISBN 0-571-19335-8

4 6 8 10 9 7 5 3

CONTENTS

Introduction, vi

THE BIG LEBOWSKI, I

INTRODUCTION: LEBOWSKI YES AND NO

The script for *The Big Lebowski* was the winner of the 1998 Bar Kochba Award, honouring achievement in the arts that defy racial and religious stereotyping and promote appreciation for the multiplicity of man. Rabbi Emmanuel Lev-Tov, the director of the Bar Kochba, is the editor of the quarterly *T'keyah* and author of the memoir *You with the Schnozz*. Upon delivering the award Rabbi Lev-Tov commended the script for its 'charming depiction of a friendship between gentile and Jew'. Praise for the script has not been universal, however. The following is excerpted from *But Is It Funny?*, an analysis of *The Big Lebowski* by Sir Anthony Forte-Bowell. Forte-Bowell is the editor of *Cinema/Not Cinema*, a journal of movie semiotics, where this essay first appeared.

> Humor may also derive from the distribution of pain among characters whose buffoonery precludes the viewer's, reader's or listener's identification. To cite a familiar example, Moe raises two fingers in a horizontal V-shape and impels them toward the eye-sockets of Curly, who interposes his upraised hand and catches the V at its apex, thereby inhibiting the fingers from achieving their end. After expressing his satisfaction through the repeated utterance of a laugh-syllable commonly rendered 'nyuk', the attention of Curly is diverted by the right hand of Moe as it flutters up to and above eye-level while the audience, though presumably not Curly, hears a high-pitched tweeting sound. While thus distracting Curly with one hand, Moe strikes him sharply in the abdomen with the other, at which the audience, though presumably not Curly, hears a strike upon a tympanum. The final 'nyuk' of Curly is thus interrupted so that he may retrieve his forcibly ejected breath, and this new breath's more gradual expulsion is so operated upon by his larynx as to form the sound commonly rendered 'ooo'. When Curly meanwhile drops the hand formerly used to parry the assault upon his eyes in order to massage his insulted midriff, Moe avails himself of the opportunity to renew his digital attack upon the

unprotected eyes, and succeeds in poking them, upon which success the audience, though presumably not Curly, hears a sound commonly associated with the release of a bent-back spring and usually rendered either 'doing' or 'ba-doing' (which sound, curiously, bears no relation to the sound that eyeballs actually give out upon being forcibly compressed). Moe will in some cases, if sufficiently angered either by Curly's smugness or by some previous evasion of a punishment deemed appropriate by Moe, so far press his advantages as to quickly and repeatedly slap both of Curly's cheeks, alternately forehand and backhand, while the audience and perhaps in this instance Curly himself (the convention here being ambiguous) hears the slapping sound amplified to an unnatural degree.

The pulling of Larry's hair will not be considered here.

I will pause to note, however, the whimsy implicit in the very name given Curly either in wry acknowledgement or in absurd refusal to acknowledge what is striking about his physical appearance, videlicet his want of hair, *et ergo a fortiori* his want of curly hair. Analysis reveals no comparable whimsy at work in the assignment of names to Larry and Moe, and an historian might here note that Lawrence and Morris were the given names of the actors by whom they were respectively depicted.

All agree that these operations, or, more to the point, their depictions, are 'funny'. What is more obscure and what even a frame-by-frame analysis of the films fails to reveal is wherein the nature of the humour resides. A similar difficulty attends analysis of the film under consideration. *The Big Lebowski* clearly harks back to films of the early 1970s that dealt with certain issues attendant to a presumed Generation Gap. In them, a youth who wears bell-bottomed trousers, beads, a shirt with a printed pattern and octagonal glasses, frequently tinted, is bedeviled by an older man wearing straight-bottomed trousers, a solid shirt, a tie with a printed pattern and curviform glasses, untinted, who 'just doesn't understand'. The more supple and intuitive intelligence of the youth is contrasted with the more linear and unimaginative intelligence of the older man, and in the end prevails over it, with the older man frequently arriving at a grudging appreciation of the youth's superior values. If the movie is of the subgenre wherein the older man will not concede the youth's superiority, then the older man shall be revealed to be a fossilized if not corrupt representative of a doomed order. *The Big Lebowski* appears to be some sort of 'spoof' upon this genre.

Repeated viewings of the movie have failed to clarify for me the genre-relevance of the themes of bowling, physical handicap, castration and the Jewish Sabbath. But perhaps we should not dismiss the possibility that they are simply authorial mistakes. Certainly the script could not be held up as a model of artistic coherence.

From *Cinema/Not Cinema*, April 1998. By permission

The Big Lebowski

Twilight. As we float up a steep, scrubby slope we hear male voices crooning 'Tumbling Tumbleweeds', and a deep, affable, Western-accented voice – Sam Elliott's, perhaps:

VOICE-OVER

A way out west there was a fella, fella I want to tell you about, fella by the name of Jeff Lebowski. At least, that was the handle his lovin' parents gave him, but he never had much use for it himself. This Lebowski, he called himself the Dude. Now Dude, that's a name no one would self-apply where I come from. But then, there was a lot about the Dude that didn't make a whole lot of sense to me. And a lot about where he lived, likewise. But then again, maybe that's why I found the place s'durned innarestin'.

We top the rise and the smoggy vastness of Los Angeles stretches before us.

. . . They call Los Angeles the City of Angels. I didn't find it to be *that* exactly, but I'll allow it as there are some nice folks there. 'Course, I can't say I seen London, and I never been to France, and I ain't never seen no queen in her damn undies, as the fella says. But I'll tell you what, after seeing Los Angeles and thisahere story I'm about to unfold – wal, I guess I seen somethin' ever' bit as stupefyin' as ya'd see in any a those other places, and in English too, so I can die with a smile on my face without feelin' like the good Lord gypped me.

INTERIOR. RALPH'S

It is late; the supermarket is all but deserted. We are tracking in on a fortyish man in Bermuda shorts and sunglasses at the dairy case. He is the Dude. His rumpled look and relaxed manner suggest a man in whom casualness runs deep.

He is feeling quarts of milk for coldness and examining their expiration dates.

VOICE-OVER

. . . Now this story I'm about to unfold took place back in the early nineties – just about the time of our conflict with Sad'm and the Eye-rackies. I only mention it 'cause sometimes there's a man – I won't say a hee-ro, 'cause what's a hee-ro? – but sometimes there's a man . . .

The Dude glances furtively about and then opens a quart of milk. He sticks his nose in the spout and sniffs.

. . . and I'm talkin' about the Dude here – sometimes there's a man who, wal, he's the man for his time'n place, he fits right in there – and that's the Dude, in Los Angeles . . .

CHECKOUT GIRL

She waits, arms folded. A small black-and-white TV next to the register shows George Bush on the White House lawn with helicopter rotors spinning behind him.

GEORGE BUSH

This aggression will not stand . . . This will not stand!

The Dude, at the little customer's lectern, interrupts his scribbling to peek over his shades. Milk beads his mustache.

VOICE-OVER

. . . and even if he's a lazy man, and the Dude was certainly that – quite possibly the laziest in Los Angeles County . . .

The Dude has his Ralph's Shopper's Club card to one side and is making out a check to Ralph's for sixty-nine cents.

. . . which would place him high in the runnin' for laziest worldwide – but sometimes there's a man . . . Sometimes there's a man . . .

EXTERIOR. RALPH'S

Long shot of the glowing Ralph's. There are only two or three cars parked in the huge lot.

VOICE-OVER

. . . wal, I lost m'train of thought here . . . but – aw hell, I done innerduced him enough.

The Dude is a small figure crossing the vast lot. Next to him walks a Mexican carry-out boy in a red apron and cap, carrying a small brown bag holding the quart of milk. The two men's footsteps echo in the still of the night.

After a walking beat the Dude offhandedly points:

DUDE

It's the Gran Torino.

BUNGALOW COURT

The Dude is going up the walkway of a small Venice bungalow court. He holds the paper sack in one hand and a small leatherette satchel in the other. He awkwardly hugs the grocery bag against his chest as he turns a key in his door.

INSIDE

The Dude enters and flicks on a light.

His head is grabbed from behind and tucked into an armpit. We track with him as he is rushed through the living room, the arm holding the satchel flailing away from his body. On entering the bedroom the outflung satchel catches a piece of door-frame and wallboard and rips through it, leaving an ovoid hole.

The Dude is propelled across the bedroom and on into a small bathroom, the satchel once again taking away a piece of door-frame. His head is plunged into the toilet. The paper bag hugged to his chest explodes milk as it hits the toilet rim and the satchel pulverizes tile as it crashes to the floor.

The Dude blows bubbles.

> VOICE
> We want that money, Lebowski. Bunny said you were good for it.

Hands haul the Dude out of the toilet. The Dude blubbers and gasps for air.

> . . . Where's the money, Lebowski?

His head is plunged back into the toilet.

> . . . Where's the money, Lebowski?

The hands haul him out again, dripping and gasping.

> . . . WHERE'S THE FUCKING MONEY, SHITHEAD?

> DUDE
> It's, uh, it's down there somewhere. Lemme take another look.

His head is plunged back in.

> VOICE
> Don't fuck with us. If your wife owes money to Jackie Treehorn, that means *you* owe money to Jackie Treehorn.

The inquisitor hauls the Dude's head out one last time and flops him

6

over so that he sits on the floor, back against the toilet. The Dude gropes back in the toilet bowl with one hand.

Looming over him is a strapping blond man.

Beyond in the living room a young Chinese man unzips his fly and walks over to a rug.

CHINESE MAN

Ever thus to deadbeats, Lebowski.

He starts peeing on the rug.

The Dude's hand comes out of the toilet bowl with his sunglasses.

DUDE

Oh, man. Don't do –

BLOND MAN

You see what happens? You see what happens, Lebowski?

The Dude puts on his dripping sunglasses.

DUDE

Look, nobody calls me Lebowski. You got the wrong guy. I'm the Dude, man.

BLOND MAN

Your name is Lebowski, Lebowski. Your wife is Bunny.

DUDE

Bunny? Look, moron . . .

He holds up his hands.

. . . You see a wedding ring? Does this place look like I'm fucking married? The toilet seat is up!

The blond man stoops to unzip the satchel. He pulls out a bowling ball and examines it in the manner of a superstitious native confronting an artifact of a more advanced civilization.

BLOND MAN

. . . The fuck is this?

The Dude pats at his pockets, takes out a joint and lights it.

DUDE

Obviously you're not a golfer.

The blond man drops the ball, which pulverizes more tile.

BLOND MAN

Woo?

The Chinese man is zipping his fly.

WOO

Yeah?

BLOND MAN

Wasn't this guy supposed to be a millionaire?

WOO

Uh?

They both look around.

. . . Fuck.

BLOND MAN

What do you think?

WOO

He looks like a fucking loser.

The Dude pulls his sunglasses down his nose with one finger and peeks over them.

DUDE

Hey. At least I'm housebroken.

The two men look at each other. They turn to leave.

WOO

Fucking waste of time.

The blond man turns testily at the door.

BLOND MAN

Thanks a lot, asshole.

On the door slam we CUT TO:

BOWLING PINS

Scattered by a strike.

Bob Dylan's 'The Man in Me' plays over, and head credits are supered upon various bowling shots. Pins fly, bowlers hoist balls, feet slide, balls glide down lanes, ball returns chuck up spinning balls, fingers slide into fingerholes, etc.

The song turns into boomy source music coming from the alley jukebox as the credits end over a clattering strike.

A lanky blond man with stringy hair tied back in a ponytail turns from the lane to walk back to the bench.

                         MAN
   Hot damn, I'm throwin' rocks tonight. Mark it, Dude.

We are tracking in on the circular bench towards a big man nursing a large plastic cup of Bud. He has dark worried eyes and a goatee. Hairy legs emerge from his khaki shorts, and a khaki army surplus shirt with cut-off sleeves serves as a vest over an old bowling shirt. This is Walter. He squints through the smoke from his own cigarette as he addresses the Dude at the scoring table.

The Dude, also holding a large plastic cup of Bud, wears some of its foam on his mustache.

                        WALTER
   This was a valued rug.

He clears his throat elaborately.

   . . . This was, uh –

                         DUDE
   Yeah man, it really tied the room together –

                        WALTER
   This was a valued, uh . . .

Donny, the strike-throwing bowler, enters and sits next to Walter.

                        DONNY
   What tied the room together, Dude?

9

WALTER

Were you listening to the story, Donny?

DONNY

What –

WALTER

Were you listening to the Dude's story?

DONNY

I was bowling –

WALTER

So you have no frame of reference, Donny. You're like a child who wanders in in the middle of a movie and wants to know –

DUDE

What's your point, Walter?

WALTER

There's no fucking reason – Here's my point, Dude – there's no fucking reason –

DONNY

Yeah Walter, what's your point?

WALTER

Huh?

DUDE

What's the point of – We all know who was at fault, so what the fuck are you talking about?

WALTER

Huh? No! What the fuck are *you* talking – I'm not – we're talking about unchecked aggression here –

DONNY

What the fuck is he talking about?

DUDE

My rug.

WALTER

Forget it, Donny. You're out of your element.

DUDE

This Chinaman who peed on my rug, I can't go give him a bill, so what the fuck are you talking about?

WALTER

What the fuck are *you* talking about?! This Chinaman is not the issue! I'm talking about drawing a line in the sand, Dude. Across this line you do not, uh – and also, Dude, Chinaman is not the preferred, uh . . . Asian–American. Please.

DUDE

Walter, this is not a guy who built the railroads, here, this is a guy who peed on my –

WALTER

What the fuck are you –

DUDE

Walter, he peed on my rug –

DONNY

He peed on the Dude's rug –

WALTER

YOU'RE OUT OF YOUR ELEMENT! This Chinaman is not the issue, Dude.

DUDE

So who –

WALTER

Jeff Lebowski. Come on. This other Jeffrey Lebowski. The millionaire. He's gonna be easier to find anyway than these two, uh . . . these two . . . And he has the wealth, uh, the resources, obviously, and there is no reason, no *fucking* reason, why his wife should go out and owe money and they pee on *your* rug. Am I wrong?

DUDE

No, but –

WALTER

Am I wrong?

DUDE

Yeah, but –

WALTER

Okay . . . That, uh . . .

He clears his throat elaborately.

. . . That rug really tied the room together, did it not?

DUDE

Fuckin' A.

DONNY

And this guy peed on it.

WALTER

Donny! Please.

DUDE

Yeah, I could find this Lebowski guy –

DONNY

His name is Lebowski? That's your name, Dude!

DUDE

Yeah, this is the guy, this guy should compensate me for the fucking rug. I mean his wife goes out and owes money and they pee on *my* rug?

WALTER

Thaaat's right Dude; they pee on your fucking rug.

A PLAQUE

We pull back from the name JEFFREY LEBOWSKI *engraved in silver to reveal that the plaque, from Variety Clubs International, honors Lebowski as* ACHIEVER OF THE YEAR.

Reflected in the plaque we see the Dude entering the room with a young man.

YOUNG MAN

And this is the study. You can see the various commendations, honorary degrees, citations of merit, et cetera.

DUDE

Yes, uh, very impressive.

YOUNG MAN

Please, feel free to inspect them.

DUDE

I'm not really, uh . . .

YOUNG MAN

Please! Please!

DUDE

Uh-huh.

We are panning the walls, looking at various citations and certificates unrelated to the ones being discussed:

YOUNG MAN

That's the key to the city of Pasadena, which Mr Lebowski was given two years ago in recognition of his various civic, uh . . .

DUDE

Uh-huh.

YOUNG MAN

That's a Los Angeles Chamber of Commerce Business Achiever award, which is given – not necessarily given every year! Given only when there's a worthy, somebody especially –

DUDE

Hey, is this him with Nancy?

YOUNG MAN

That is indeed Mr Lebowski with the First Lady, yes, taken
when –

DUDE

Lebowski on the right?

YOUNG MAN

Of course, Mr Lebowski on the right, Mrs Reagan on the
left, taken when –

DUDE

He's handicapped, huh?

YOUNG MAN

Mr Lebowski is disabled, yes. And this picture was taken
when Mrs Reagan was First Lady of the nation, yes, yes?
Not of California.

DUDE

Far out.

YOUNG MAN

And in fact he met privately with the President, though
unfortunately there wasn't time for a photo opportunity.

DUDE

Nancy's pretty good.

YOUNG MAN

Wonderful woman. We were very –

DUDE

Are these . . .

YOUNG MAN

These are Mr Lebowski's children, so to speak –

DUDE

Different mothers, huh?

YOUNG MAN

No, they –

DUDE

I guess he's pretty, uh, racially pretty cool –

YOUNG MAN

They're not his, heh-heh, they're not literally his children;
they're the Little Lebowski Urban Achievers, inner-city
children of promise but without the –

DUDE

I see.

YOUNG MAN

– without the means for higher education, so Mr Lebowski
has committed to sending all of them to college.

DUDE

Jeez. Think he's got room for one more?

YOUNG MAN

One – oh! Heh-heh. You never went to college?

DUDE

Well, yeah I did, but I spent most of my time occupying
various, um, administration buildings –

YOUNG MAN

Heh-heh –

DUDE

– smoking Thai-stick, breaking into the ROTC –

YOUNG MAN

Yes, heh –

DUDE

– and bowling. I'll tell you the truth, Brandt, I don't
remember most of it – Jeez! Fuck me!

Our continuing track has brought us onto a framed Time Magazine
cover which is headlined: ARE YOU A LEBOWSKI ACHIEVER? *Oddly,
the Dude's sunglassed face is on it; we realize that, under the
magazine's logo and headline, the display is mirrored.*

*We hear the door open and the whine of a motor. The Dude, wearing
shorts and a bowling shirt, turns to look.*

So does Brandt, his escort. Brandt wears a suit and has his hands clasped smartly in front of his groin.

Entering the room is a fat sixtyish man in a motorized wheelchair – Jeffrey Lebowski.

LEBOWSKI
Okay, sir, you're a Lebowski, I'm a Lebowski, that's terrific. I'm very busy, so what can I do for you?

He wheels himself behind a desk. The Dude sits facing him, and Brandt withdraws.

DUDE
Well, sir, it's this rug I have, it really tied the room together –

LEBOWSKI
You told Brandt on the phone, he told me. So where do I fit in?

DUDE
Well they were looking for you, these two guys, they were trying to –

LEBOWSKI
I'll say it again, all right? You told Brandt. He told me. I know what happened. Yes? Yes?

DUDE
So you know they were trying to piss on *your* rug –

LEBOWSKI
Did I urinate on your rug?

DUDE
You mean, did you personally come and pee on my –

LEBOWSKI
Hello! Do you speak English? *Parla usted Inglese?* I'll say it again. Did I urinate on your rug?

DUDE
Well no, like I said, Woo peed on the rug –

LEBOWSKI

Hello! Hello! So every time – I just want to understand this, sir – every time a rug is micturated upon in this fair city, I have to compensate the –

DUDE

Come on, man, I'm not trying to scam anybody here, I'm just –

LEBOWSKI

You're just looking for a handout like every other – Are you employed, Mr Lebowski?

DUDE

Look, let me explain something. I'm not Mr Lebowski; *you're* Mr Lebowski. I'm the Dude. So that's what you call me. That, or Duder. His Dudeness. Or El Duderino, if, you know, you're not into the whole brevity thing –

LEBOWSKI

Are you employed, sir?

DUDE

. . . Employed?

LEBOWSKI

You don't go out and make a living dressed like *that* in the middle of a weekday.

DUDE

Is this a – what day is this?

LEBOWSKI

But I *do* work, so if you don't mind –

DUDE

No, look. I do mind. The Dude minds. This will not stand, ya know, this will not stand, man. I mean, if your wife owes –

LEBOWSKI

My wife is not the issue here. I hope that my wife will someday learn to live on her allowance, which is ample, but if she doesn't, *sir*, that will be *her* problem, not mine, just as your rug is *your* problem, just as every *bum's* lot in life is his own responsibility regardless of whom he chooses to blame. I didn't blame anyone for the loss of my legs, some Chinaman in Korea *took* them from me, but I went out and achieved anyway. I can't solve your problems, sir, only you can.

The Dude rises.

DUDE

Ah, fuck it.

LEBOWSKI

Sure! Fuck it! That's your answer! Tattoo it on your forehead! Your answer to everything!

The Dude is heading for the door.

. . . Your 'revolution' is over, Mr Lebowski! Condolences! The bums lost!

As the Dude opens the door:

. . . My advice is, do what your parents did! Get a job, sir! The bums will always lose – do you hear me, Lebowski? THE BUMS WILL ALWAYS –

The Dude shuts the door on the old man's bellowing to find himself –

HALLWAY

– in a high coffered hallway. Brandt is approaching.

BRANDT

How was your meeting, Mr Lebowski?

DUDE

Okay. The old man told me to take any rug in the house.

WALKWAY

A houseman with a rolled-up carpet on one shoulder goes down a stone walk that winds through the back lawn, past a swimming pool, to a multi-car garage. Brandt and the Dude follow.

BRANDT

Manolo will load it into your car for you, uh, Dude.

DUDE

It's the Gran Torino.

The Dude's point of view, tracking toward the pool, shows a young woman who sits facing it, her back to us. She is leaning forward to paint her toenails.

Beyond her a black form floats in an inflatable chair in the pool.

BRANDT

Well, enjoy, and perhaps we'll see you again some time, Dude.

DUDE

Yeah sure, if I'm ever in the neighborhood, need to use the john . . .

We close in on the woman and arc around her foot as she finishes painting the nails emerald green.

The Dude looks.

The young woman – in her early twenties – looks up.

She leans back and extends her leg toward the Dude.

YOUNG WOMAN

Blow on them.

The Dude pulls his sunglasses down his nose to peek over them.

DUDE

. . . Huh?

She waggles her foot and giggles.

YOUNG WOMAN

G'ahead. Blow.

The Dude tentatively grabs hold of the offered foot.

DUDE

You want me to blow on your toes?

YOUNG WOMAN

Uh-huh . . . I can't blow that far.

The Dude looks over at the pool.

DUDE

. . . You sure he won't mind?

The man bobbing in the inflatable chair is passed out. He is thin, in his thirties, with long stringy blond hair. He wears black leather pants and a black leather jacket, open, shirtless, exposing fine blond chest hair and pale skin. One arm trails off into the water; next to it, an empty whiskey bottle bobs.

YOUNG WOMAN

Uli doesn't care about anything. He's a nihilist.

DUDE

. . . Practicing?

The young woman smiles.

YOUNG WOMAN

You're not blowing.

Brandt nervously takes the Dude by the elbow.

BRANDT

Our guest has to be getting along, Mrs Lebowski.

The Dude reluctantly allows himself to be led away, still looking at the young woman.

DUDE

You're Bunny?

BUNNY

I'll suck your cock for a thousand dollars.

Brandt releases a hurricane of forced laughter:

BRANDT

Ha-ha-ha-ha! Wonderful woman. Very free-spirited. We're all very fond of her.

BUNNY

Brandt can't watch though. Or he has to pay a hundred.

Ha-ha-ha-ha-ha! That's marvelous.

He continues to pull away the Dude, who looks back over his shoulder:

DUDE

I'm just gonna find a cash machine.

BOWLING PINS

Scattered by a strike.

Donny calls out from the bench:

DONNY

Grasshopper Dude – They're dead in the water!

As the Dude walks back to the scoring table he turns to another team sharing the lane.

DUDE

Your maples, Carl.

Walter, just arriving, is carrying a leatherette satchel in one hand and a large plastic carrier in the other.

WALTER

Way to go, Dude. If you will it, it is no dream.

DUDE

You're fucking twenty minutes late. What the fuck is that?

WALTER

Theodore Herzcl.

DUDE

Huh?

WALTER

State of Israel. If you will it, Dude, it is no –

DUDE

What the fuck're you talking about? The carrier. What's in the fucking carrier?

WALTER

Huh? Oh – Cynthia's Pomeranian. Can't leave him home alone or he eats the furniture.

DUDE

What the fuck are you –

WALTER

I'm saying, Cynthia's Pomeranian. I'm looking after it while Cynthia and Marty Ackerman are in Hawaii.

DUDE

You brought a fucking Pomeranian bowling?

WALTER

What do you mean 'brought it bowling'? I didn't rent it shoes. I'm not buying it a fucking beer. He's not gonna take your fucking turn, Dude.

He lets the small yapping dog out of the carrier. It scoots around the bowling table, sniffing at bowlers and wagging its tail.

DUDE

Hey, man, if *my* fucking ex-wife asked *me* to take care of her fucking dog while she and her boyfriend went to Honolula, I'd tell her to go fuck herself. Why can't she board it?

WALTER

First of all, Dude, you don't have an ex; secondly, it's a fucking show dog with fucking papers. You can't board it. It gets upset, its hair falls out.

DUDE

Hey man –

WALTER

Fucking dog has papers, Dude – Over the line!

Smokey turns from his last roll to look at Walter.

SMOKEY

Huh?

WALTER

Over the line, Smokey! I'm sorry. That's a foul.

SMOKEY

Bullshit. Eight, Dude.

WALTER

Excuse me! Mark it zero. Next frame.

SMOKEY

Bullshit. Walter!

WALTER

This is not 'Nam. This is bowling. There are rules.

DUDE

Come on Walter, it's just – it's Smokey. So his toe slipped over a little, it's just a game.

WALTER

This is a *league* game. This determines who enters the next round robin, am I wrong?

SMOKEY

Yeah, but –

WALTER

Am I wrong!?

SMOKEY

Yeah, but I wasn't over. Gimme the marker, Dude, I'm marking it an eight.

Walter takes out a gun.

WALTER

Smokey my friend, you're entering a world of pain.

DUDE

Hey Walter –

WALTER

Mark that frame an eight, you're entering a world of pain.

SMOKEY

I'm not –

WALTER

A world of pain.

SMOKEY

. . . Look, Dude, I don't hold with this. This guy is your
partner, you should –

Walter primes the gun and points it at Smokey's head.

WALTER

HAS THE WHOLE WORLD GONE CRAZY? AM I THE ONLY ONE HERE
WHO GIVES A SHIT ABOUT THE RULES? MARK IT ZERO!

*The Pomeranian is excitedly yapping at Walter's elbow, making high,
tail-wagging, body-twisting leaps.*

DUDE

Walter, they're calling the cops, put the piece away.

WALTER

MARK IT ZERO!

26

SMOKEY

Walter –

WALTER

YOU THINK I'M FUCKING AROUND HERE? MARK IT ZERO!!

SMOKEY

All right! There it is! It's fucking zero!

He points frantically at the score projected above the lane.

. . . You happy, you crazy fuck?

WALTER

This is a league game, Smokey.

PARKING LOT

Walter and the Dude walk to the Dude's car. The Pomeranian trots happily behind Walter, who totes the empty carrier.

DUDE

Walter, you can't do that. These guys're like me, they're pacifists. Smokey was a conscientious objector.

WALTER

You know, Dude, I myself dabbled with pacifism at one point. Not in 'Nam, of course –

DUDE

And you *know* Smokey has emotional problems!

WALTER

You mean – beyond pacifism?

DUDE

He's fragile, man! He's very fragile!

As the two men get into the car:

WALTER

Huh. I did not know that. Well, it's water under the bridge. And we do enter the next round robin, am I wrong?

DUDE

No, you're not wrong –

WALTER

Am I wrong!

DUDE

You're not wrong, Walter, you're just an asshole.

They watch a squad car take a squealing turn into the lot.

WALTER

Okay then. We play Quintana and O'Brien next week.
They'll be pushovers.

DUDE

Just, just take it easy, Walter.

WALTER

That's your answer to everything, Dude. And let me point
out, pacifism is not – look at our current situation with that
camel-fucker in Iraq – pacifism is not something to hide
behind.

DUDE

Well, just take it easy, man.

WALTER

I'm perfectly calm, Dude.

DUDE

Yeah? Wavin' a gun around?!

WALTER

Calmer than you are.

DUDE

Just take it easy, man!

WALTER

Calmer than you are.

DUDE'S HOUSE

*A large, brilliant Persian rug lies beneath the Dude's beat-up old
furniture.*

At a table next to an answering machine the Dude is mixing kalhua, vodka and milk.

VOICE

Dude, this is Smokey. Look, I don't wanna be a hard-on about this, and I know it wasn't your fault, but I just thought it was fair to tell you that Gene and I will be submitting this to the League and asking them to set aside the round. Or maybe forfeit it to us –

DUDE

Shit!

VOICE

– so, like I say, just thought, you know, fair warning. Tell Walter.

A beep.

ANOTHER VOICE

Mr Lebowski, this is Brandt at, uh, well – at Mr Lebowski's office. Please call us as soon as is convenient.

Beep.

ANOTHER VOICE

Mr Lebowski, this is Fred Dynarski with the Southern Cal Bowling League. I just got a, an informal report, uh, that a, uh, a member of your team, uh, Walter Sobchak, drew a *firearm* during league play –

We hear the doorbell.

THE DOOR

It swings open to reveal a short, balding middle-aged man in a black T-shirt and black cut-off jeans.

MAN

Dude.

DUDE

Hiya, Marty.

MARTY

...de, I finally got the venue I wanted. I'm performing my
...ance quintet – you know, my cycle – at Crane Jackson's
Fountain Street Theater on Tuesday night, and I'd love it if
you came and gave me notes.

The Dude takes a swig of his White Russian.

DUDE

Sure, Marty, I'll be there.

MARTY

... Dude, uh, tomorrow is already the tenth.

DUDE

Uh-huh.

MARTY

Just, uh, just slip the rent under my door.

DUDE

Yeah, okay.

BACK IN THE LIVING ROOM

The voice continues on the machine:

VOICE

– serious infraction, and examine your standing. Thank you.

Beep.

VOICE

Mr Lebowski, Brandt again. Please do call us when you get
in and I'll send the limo. Let me assure you – I hope you're
not avoiding this call because of the rug, which, I assure
you, is not a problem. We need your help and, uh – well,
we would very much like to see you. Thank you. It's Brandt.

TRACKING

*We are pushing Brandt down the high-ceilinged hallway. Distantly,
we hear a dolorous soprano. Brandt talks back over his shoulder:*

BRANDT

We've had some terrible news. Mr Lebowski is in seclusion in the West Wing.

DUDE

Huh.

Brandt throws open a pair of heavy double doors. The Wagnerian music washes over us as we enter a great study where Jeffrey Lebowski, a blanket thrown over his knees, stares hauntedly into a fire.

Brandt announces, ambiguously:

BRANDT

Mr Lebowski.

Jeffrey Lebowski waves the Dude in without looking around.

LEBOWSKI

. . . It's funny. I can look back on a life of achievement, on challenges met, competitors bested, obstacles overcome . . . I've accomplished more than most men, and without the use of my legs. What . . . What makes a man, Mr Lebowski?

DUDE

Dude.

LEBOWSKI

. . . Huh?

DUDE

I don't know, sir.

LEBOWSKI

Is it . . . is it, being prepared to do the right thing? Whatever the price? Isn't that what makes a man?

DUDE

That, and a pair of testicles.

Lebowski turns away from the Dude with a haunted stare, lost in thought.

LEBOWSKI

... You're joking. But perhaps you're right ...

The Dude thumps at his chest pocket.

DUDE

Mind if I smoke a jay?

LEBOWSKI

... Bunny ...

The firelight shows tear-tracks on his cheeks.

DUDE

'Scuse me?

LEBOWSKI

... Bunny Lebowski ... She is the light of my life. Are you surprised at my tears, sir?

DUDE

Fuckin' A.

LEBOWSKI

Strong men also cry ... Strong men also cry ...

He clears his throat.

... I received this fax this morning.

Brandt hastily pulls a flimsy sheet from his clipboard and hands it to the Dude.

... As you can see, it is a ransom note. Sent by cowards. Men who are unable to achieve on a level field of play. Men who will not sign their names. Weaklings. Bums.

The Dude examines the fax:

WE HAVE BUNNY. GATHER ONE MILLION DOLLARS IN UNMARKED NON-CONSECUTIVE TWENTIES. AWAIT INSTRUCTIONS. NO FUNNY STUFF.

DUDE

Bummer.

Lebowski looks soulfully at the Dude.

. . . Brandt will fill you in on the details.

He turns to gaze once again into the fire. Brandt tugs at the Dude's shirt and points him back to the hall.

HALLWAY

The soprano's singing is once again faint. Brandt's voice is hushed:

BRANDT
Mr Lebowski is prepared to make a generous offer to you to act as courier once we get instructions for the money.

DUDE
Why me, man?

BRANDT
He suspects that the culprits might be the very people who, uh, soiled your rug, and you're in a unique position to confirm or, uh, disconfirm that suspicion.

DUDE
So he thinks it's the carpet-pissers, huh?

BRANDT
Well, Dude, we just don't know.

BOWLING PINS

CRASH – scattered by a strike, in slow motion.

REVERSE: A tall, thin, Hispanic bowler displays perfect form, still in slow motion. He wears an all-in-one dacron–polyester stretch bowling outfit with a racing stripe down each side.

NEARBY

The Dude sits next to Walter, watching the bowler.

DUDE
Fucking Quintana – that creep can roll, man . . .

*We go back to the Hispanic bowler as the Dude and Walter's
conversation continues over:*

                    WALTER
Yeah, but he's a fucking pervert, Dude.

                    DUDE
Huh?

                    WALTER
Your man is a sex offender. With a record. Spent six months
in Chino for exposing himself to an eight-year-old.

FLASHBACK

*We see Quintana, in pressed jeans and a stretchy sweater, walking up
a stoop in a residential neighborhood and ringing the bell. The
conversation continues as voice-over:*

                    DUDE
Huh.

35

WALTER

When he moved down to Venice he had to go door-to-door to tell everyone he's a pederast.

The door swings open and a beer-swilling middle-aged man looks dully out at Quintana.

DONNY

What's a pederast, Walter?

WALTER

Shut the fuck up, Donny.

QUINTANA

Back in the lane, he wheels from a strike and thrusts a black-gloved fist into the air. Stitched above the breast pocket of his all-in-one is his first name, 'Jesus'.

Walter and the Dude have now been joined by Donny.

WALTER

Anyway. How much they offer you?

DUDE

Twenty grand. And of course I still keep the rug.

WALTER

Just for making the hand-off?

DUDE

Yeah . . .

He slips a little black box out of his shirt pocket.

. . . They gave Dude a beeper, so whenever these guys call –

WALTER

What if it's during a game?

DUDE

I told him if it was during league play –

DONNY

If what's during league play?

WALTER

Life does not stop and start at your convenience, you miserable piece of shit.

DONNY

What's wrong with Walter, Dude?

DUDE

I figure it's easy money, it's all pretty harmless. I mean she probably kidnapped herself.

WALTER

Huh?

DONNY

What do you mean, Dude?

DUDE

Rug-peers did not do this. I mean, look at it. Young trophy wife. Marries a guy for money but figures he isn't giving her enough. She owes money all over town –

37

WALTER

That . . . fucking . . . bitch!

DUDE

It's all a goddamn fake. Like Lenin said, look for the person who will benefit. And you will, uh, you know, you'll, uh, you know what I'm trying to say –

DONNY

I am the Walrus.

WALTER

That fucking bitch!

DUDE

Yeah.

DONNY

I am the Walrus.

WALTER

Shut the fuck up, Donny! *V. I.* Lenin! Vladimir Ilyich *Uly*anov!

DONNY

What the fuck is he talking about?

WALTER

That's fucking *exactly* what happened, Dude! That makes me fucking *sick!*

DUDE

Yeah, well, what do you care, Walter?

DONNY

Yeah Dude, why is Walter so pissed off?

WALTER

Those rich fucks! This whole fucking thing – I did not watch my buddies die face down in the muck so that this fucking *strumpet* –

DUDE

I don't see any connection to Vietnam, Walter.

WALTER

Well, there isn't a *literal* connection, Dude.

DUDE

Walter, face it, there isn't *any* connection. It's your roll.

WALTER

Have it your way. The point is –

DUDE

It's your roll –

WALTER

The fucking point is –

DUDE

It's your roll.

VOICE

Are you ready to be fucked, man?

They both look up.

Quintana looks down from the lip of the lanes. Over his all-in-one he now wears a windbreaker with a racing stripe and 'Jesus' stitched on the breast. He is holding a fancy black-and-red leather ball satchel. Behind him stands his partner, O'Brien, a short fat Irishman with tufted red hair.

QUINTANA

I see you rolled your way into the semis. Deos mio, man. Seamus and me, we're gonna fuck you up.

DUDE

Yeah well, that's just, ya know, like, your opinion, man.

Quintana now addresses Walter:

QUINTANA

Let me tell *you* something, pendejo. You pull any your crazy shit with us, you flash a piece out on the lanes, I'll take it away from you and stick it up your ass and pull the fucking trigger till it goes 'click'.

39

DUDE

Jesus.

QUINTANA

You said it, man. Nobody fucks with the Jesus.

He walks away. Walter nods sadly.

WALTER

. . . Eight-year-olds, Dude.

DUDE'S BUNGALOW

We are looking down at the Dude who lies on his back on the Persian rug. His eyes are closed. He wears a Walkman headset. We can just hear an intermittent clatter leaking tinnily through the headphones.

In his outflung hand lies a cassette case labeled VENICE BEACH LEAGUE PLAYOFFS *1987.*

The Dude absently licks his lips as we faintly hear a ball rumbling down the lane. On its impact with the pins, the Dude opens his eyes.

A blonde woman looms over him. Next to her a young man in paint-spattered denims stoops and swings something toward the camera.

The Dude screams.

The sap catches him on the chin and sends his head thunking back onto the rug.

A million stars explode against a field of black.

We hear the 'La-la-la-las' of 'The Man in Me'.

The black field dissolves into the pattern of the rug. The rug rolls away to reveal an aerial view of the city of Los Angeles at twilight moving below us at great speed.

The Dude is flying over the city, his arms thrown out in front of him, the wind whipping his hair and billowing his bowling shirt. He looks up.

Ahead, the mysterious blonde woman flies away, riding on the Dude's rug like a sheik on a magic carpet. She is outpacing us, becoming smaller.

The Dude does a couple of lazy crawl strokes and then notices that a bowling ball has materialized in his forward hand. His bemusement turns to concern over the aerodynamic implications just as the ball seems to assume weight suddenly, snapping his arm down, and him after it.

He is falling.

From a high angle we see the Dude hurtling down toward the city, dragged by the ball.

A reverse, looking up, shows the Dude hurtling toward us out of the inky sky, his eyes wide with horror. Led by the bowling ball, he zooms past the camera to leave us in black.

We hear a distant rumble, like thunder. Dull reflections materialize in the darkness.

They are glints off the shiny surface of an oncoming bowling ball, and we pull back, showing the blackness to be the inside of a ball return. The gleaming ball that it regurgitates is overtaking us.

The Dude, tiny now, and standing on the chrome track of the ball return, looks up, up, up at the looming ball, its mass rolling a huge shadow across his face.

The gleaming ball shows three dead black holes rolling toward us – finger holes.

The largest – the thumb hole – rolls directly over us, to engulf us once again in black.

The black rolls away and we are spinning – spinning down a bowling lane – our point of view is that of someone trapped in the thumb hole of the rolling ball.

We see the receding bowler spinning away. It is the blonde woman performing her follow-through.

Floor spins up at us and then away; ceiling spins up and away; the length of the alley with pins at the far end; floor; ceiling; approaching pins; again and again.

We hit the pins and clatter into blackness. We hear pins ricochet and echo.

We hear an irritating, insistent beeping.

FADE IN

We are close on the Dude, upside-down. As the picture fades in, the bowling noises continue, but filtered and faint. They come from the Dude's Walkman, the headset of which is now askew, with one arm off his ear.

As the Dude opens his eyes we spiral slowly upward to put him right side around. His head is now resting against hardwood floor, not rug.

DUDE

Oh man . . .

He raises himself onto his elbows and massages the red lump on his jaw. The beeper on his belt is blinking red in sync with the continuing irritating beeps.

Widening out on the room shows an overturned end table, but otherwise the furniture is in place.

The rug is gone.

The Dude looks around. The bowling sounds continue. The beeps continue.

The phone starts to jangle.

TRACK

We push Brandt down the familiar marble hallway. Again there is a distant aria. Brandt throws out a wrist to consult his watch.

> BRANDT
> They called about eighty minutes ago. They want you to take the money and drive north on the 405. They'll call you on the portable phone with instructions in about forty minutes. One person only or I'd go with you. They were very clear on that: one person only. What happened to your jaw?

> DUDE
> Oh, nothin', you know . . .

They have reached a small desk outside of the Big Lebowski's office; Brandt opens its bottom drawer with a key and takes out an attaché case. He hands this to the Dude along with a cellular phone in a battery-pack carrying case.

> BRANDT
> Here's the money, and the phone. Please, Dude, follow whatever instructions they give.

> DUDE
> Uh-huh.

> BRANDT
> Her life is in your hands.

> DUDE
> Oh, man, don't say that.

> BRANDT
> Mr Lebowski asked me to repeat that: Her life is in your hands.

43

DUDE

Shit.

BRANDT

Her life is in your hands, Dude. And report back to us as soon as it's done.

DUDE'S CAR

We pan off the Dude driving, to his point of view through the windshield. The headlights play over Walter waiting in front of the store-front of SOBCHAK SECURITY. *Though he is wearing khaki shorts and shirt, the fact that he holds a battered brown briefcase makes him look oddly like a commuter. He also holds an irregular shape bundled in brown wrapping paper.*

The car stops in front of him and he opens the Dude's door and hands in the briefcase.

WALTER

Take the ringer. I'll drive.

The Dude takes the briefcase and slides over.

DUDE

The what?

WALTER

The ringer! The ringer, Dude! Have they called yet?

The Dude opens the briefcase and paws bemusedly through it as the car starts rolling.

DUDE

What the hell is this?

WALTER

My dirty undies. Laundry, Dude. The whites.

DUDE

Agh –

He closes the briefcase.

. . . Walter, I'm sure there's a reason you brought your dirty undies –

WALTER

Thaaaat's right, Dude. The weight. The ringer can't look
empty.

DUDE

Walter – what the fuck are you thinking?

WALTER

Well you're right, Dude, I got to thinking. I got to thinking
why should we settle for a measly fucking twenty grand –

DUDE

We? What the fuck we? You said you just wanted to come
along –

WALTER

My point, Dude, is why should we settle for twenty grand
when we can keep the entire million. Am I wrong?

DUDE

Yes, you're wrong. This isn't a fucking game, Walter –

WALTER

It is a fucking game, you said so yourself, Dude – she
kidnapped herself –

DUDE

Yeah, but –

The phone chirps.

The Dude grabs it.

Dude here.

VOICE
(*German accent*)

. . . Who is this?

DUDE

Dude the Bagman, man. Where do you want us to go?

VOICE

. . . *Us?*

DUDE

Shit . . . Uh, yeah, you know, me and the driver. I'm not handling the money and driving the car and talking on the phone all by my fucking –

VOICE

Shut the fuck up.

Beat.

. . . Hello?

DUDE

Yeah?

VOICE

Okay, listen –

WALTER

Dude, are you fucking this up?

VOICE

Who is that?

DUDE

The driver man, I told you –

Click. Dial tone.

. . . Oh shit. Walter, he . . .

WALTER

What the fuck is going on there?

DUDE

They hung up, Walter! You fucked it up! You fucked it up! Her life was in our hands!

WALTER

Easy, Dude.

DUDE

We're screwed now! We don't get shit and they're gonna kill her! We're fucked, Walter!

WALTER

Dude, nothing is fucked. Come on. You're being very un-Dude. They'll call back. Look, she kidnapped her –

The phone chirps.

. . . Ya see? Nothing is fucked up here, Dude. Nothing is fucked. These guys are fucking amateurs –

DUDE

Shut up, Walter! Don't fucking say peep when I'm doing business here.

WALTER
(*patronizing*)

Okay Dude. Have it your way.

The Dude unclips the phone from the battery pack.

. . . But they're amateurs.

The Dude glares at Walter. Into the phone:

DUDE

Dude here.

VOICE

. . . Okay, vee proceed. But only if there is no funny stuff.

DUDE

Yeah.

VOICE

So no funny stuff. Okay?

DUDE

Hey, just tell me where the fuck you want us to go.

A HIGHWAY SIGN: SIMI VALLEY ROAD

It flashes by in the headlights of the roaring car.

DUDE

That was the sign.

Walter wrestles the car onto the two-lane road.

47

WALTER

Yeah. So as long as we get her back, nobody's in a position to complain. And we keep the baksheesh.

DUDE

Terrific, Walter, but you haven't told me how we get her back. Where is she?

WALTER

That's the simple part, Dude. When we make the hand-off, I grab the guy and beat it out of him.

He looks at the Dude.

. . . Huh?

DUDE

Yeah. That's a great plan, Walter. That's fucking ingenious, if I understand it correctly. That's a Swiss fucking watch.

WALTER

Thaaat's right, Dude. The beauty of this is its simplicity. If the plan gets too complex something always goes wrong. If there's one thing I learned in 'Nam –

The phone chirps.

DUDE

Dude.

VOICE

You are approaching vooden britch. When you cross it you srow ze bag from ze left vindow of ze moving kar. Do not slow down. Vee vatch you.

Click. Dial tone.

DUDE

Fuck.

WALTER

What'd he say? Where's the hand-off?

DUDE

There is no fucking hand-off, Walter! At a wooden bridge we throw the money out of the car!

WALTER

Huh?

DUDE

We throw the money out of the moving car!

Walter stares dumbly.

WALTER

. . . We can't do that, Dude. That fucks up our plan.

DUDE

Well call them up and explain it to 'em, Walter! Your plan
is so fucking simple, I'm sure they'd fucking understand it!
That's the beauty of it, Walter!

WALTER

Wooden bridge, huh?

DUDE

I'm throwing the money, Walter! We're not fucking around!

WALTER

The bridge is coming up! Gimme the ringer, Dude! Chop-chop!

DUDE

Fuck that! I love you, Walter, but sooner or later you're
gonna have to face the fact that you're a goddamn moron.

WALTER

Okay, Dude, no time to argue. Here's the bridge –

*There is the bump and new steady of the car on the bridge. The Dude
is twisting around to pull the money briefcase from the back seat.
Walter reaches one arm across Dude's body to grab the laundry.*

. . . and here goes the ringer.

He flings it out the window.

DUDE

Walter!

WALTER

Your wheel, Dude! I'm rolling out!

DUDE

What the fuck?!

WALTER

Your wheel! At fifteen em-pee-aitch I roll out! I double back, grab one of 'em and beat it out of him! The Uzi!

DUDE

. . . Uzi?

Walter points across the seat at the paper-wrapped bundle.

WALTER

You didn't think I was rolling out of here naked!

DUDE

Walter, please –

Walter has flung open his door and is leaning out over the road.

WALTER

Fifteen! This is it, Dude! Let's take that hill!

Walter rolls out with his parcel, grunting loudly as he hits the pavement. The car swerves and lurches and the Dude, cursing, takes the wheel.

OUTSIDE

Walter tumbles onto the shoulder and – RAT-TAT-TAT-TAT! *– muzzle flashes tear open the wrapping paper.*

INSIDE THE CAR

The car rocks and the Dude wrestles with the wheel.

OUTSIDE

Chinking bullet hits walk across the car body and blow a rear tire.

The car slues around into skid.

INSIDE

The Dude is thrown forward as the car hits something.

OUTSIDE

*The front of his car is crumpled into a tree. The car body sags back
to the left, where the rear wheel has been shot out. The Dude struggles
out holding the satchel of money.*

Walter is just rising from the ground, massaging an injured knee.

*The Dude runs up the road toward the bridge, frantically waving the
satchel in the air.*

> DUDE
> WE HAVE IT! WE HAVE IT!

*There is a distant engine roar. A motorcycle bumps up onto the road
from the ravine under the bridge and, tires squealing, skids around
to speed away in the opposite direction. It is closely followed by two
more roaring motorcycles.*

WE HAVE IT! . . . We have it!

*The Dude and Walter stand in the middle of the road, watching the
three red tail lights fishtail away.*

After a long staring silence:

> WALTER
> . . . Ahh fuck it. Let's go bowling.

BOWLING LANE

A ball rumbles in to scatter ten pins.

*Walter turns from the lane to join the Dude in the nook of molded
plastic chairs. The Dude listlessly holds the portable phone in his lap.
It is ringing.*

> WALTER
> Aitz chaim he, Dude. As the ex used to say.

> DUDE
> What the fuck is that supposed to mean? What the fuck're
> we gonna tell Lebowski?

51

WALTER

Huh? Oh, him, yeah. Well I don't see, um – what exactly is
the problem?

The portable phone stops ringing.

DUDE

Huh? The problem is – what do you mean what's the –
there's no – we didn't – they're gonna kill that poor woman!

WALTER

What the fuck're you talking about? That poor woman – that
poor *slut* – kidnapped herself, Dude. You said so yourself –

DUDE

No, Walter! I said I *thought* she kidnapped herself! You're
the one who's so fucking certain –

WALTER

That's right, Dude, hundred percent certain –

Donny trots up excitedly:

DONNY

They posted the next round of the tournament –

WALTER

Donny, shut the f – when do we play?

DONNY

This Saturday. Quintana and –

WALTER

Saturday! Well they'll have to reschedule.

DUDE

Walter, what'm I gonna tell Lebowski?

WALTER

I told that fuck down at the league office – Who's in charge
of scheduling?

DUDE

Walter –

DONNY

Burkhalter.

WALTER

I told that Kraut a fucking thousand times I don't roll on
shabbas.

DONNY

It's already posted.

WALTER

WELL THEY CAN FUCKING UN-POST IT!

DUDE

Who gives a shit, Walter? What about that poor woman?
What do we tell –

WALTER

C'mon Dude, eventually she'll get sick of her little game
and, you know, wander back –

DONNY

How come you don't roll on Saturday, Walter?

WALTER

I'm shomer shabbas.

DONNY

What's that, Walter?

DUDE

Yeah, and in the meantime what do I tell Lebowski?

WALTER

Saturday is shabbas. Jewish day of rest. Means I don't work,
I don't drive a car, I don't fucking *ride* in a car, I don't handle
money, I don't turn on the oven, and I sure as shit don't
fucking roll!

DONNY

Sheesh.

DUDE

Walter, how –

WALTER

Shomer shabbas.

The Dude gets to his feet.

DUDE

That's it. I'm out of here.

WALTER

For Christ's sake, Dude . . .

Walter and Donny join the Dude as he walks out of the bowling alley.

. . . Hell, you just tell him – Well, you tell him, uh, we made the hand-off, everything went, uh, you know –

DONNY

Oh yeah, how'd it go?

WALTER

Went all right. Dude's car got a little dinged up –

DUDE

But Walter, we didn't make the fucking hand-off! They didn't get the fucking money and they're gonna – they're gonna –

WALTER

Yeah yeah, 'kill that poor woman'.

He waves both arms as if conducting a symphony orchestra.

. . . Kill that poor woman.

DONNY

Walter, if you can't ride in a car, how d'you get around on Shammas –

WALTER

Really, Dude, you surprise me. They're not gonna kill shit. They're not gonna *do* shit. What can they do? Fuckin' amateurs. And meanwhile, look at the bottom line. Who's sitting on a million fucking dollars? Am I wrong?

Walter –

WALTER

Who's got a fucking million fucking dollars parked in the trunk of our car out here?

DUDE

'Our' car, Walter?

WALTER

And what do they got, Dude? My dirty undies. My fucking whites. Say, where *is* the car?

The three bowlers, stopped at the edge of the lot, stare at an empty parking space.

DONNY

... *Who* has your undies, Walter?

WALTER

Where's your car, Dude?

DUDE

You don't know, Walter? You seem to know the answer to
everything else!

WALTER

Hmm. Well, we were in a handicapped spot. It, uh, it was
probably towed.

DUDE

It's been stolen, Walter! You fucking know it's been stolen!

WALTER

Well, that's not a given, Dude –

DUDE

Aw, fuck it . . .

*The Dude walks away across the lot. The portable phone starts ringing
again.*

DONNY

Where you going, Dude?

DUDE

I'm going home, Donny.

DONNY

Your phone's ringing, Dude.

DUDE

Thank you, Donny.

DUDE'S LIVING ROOM

*The Dude is slumped back disconsolately in his easy chair, fingers of
one hand cupped over his sunglasses. Facing him on the couch are
two uniformed policemen, one middle-aged, the other a fresh-faced
rookie.*

*At the cut, the portable phone in the Dude's lap is chirping. The Dude
waits for the rings to end.*

When they do:

                        DUDE
. . . 1973 Gran Torino.

                    YOUNGER COP
Color?

                        DUDE
Green. Some brown, or, uh, rust, coloration.

                    YOUNGER COP
And was there anything of value *in* the car?

                        DUDE
Huh? Oh. Yeah. Tape deck. Couple of Creedence tapes. And
there was a, uh . . . my briefcase.

                    YOUNGER COP
In the briefcase?

                        DUDE
Papers. Just papers. You know, my papers. Business papers.

                    YOUNGER COP
And what do you do, sir?

                        DUDE
I'm unemployed.

                    OLDER COP
. . . Most people, we're working nights, they offer us coffee.

*There is silence. The Dude continues to stare at a spot on the floor.
The older cop stares at him.*

. . . Me, I don't drink coffee. But it's nice when they offer.

At length:

                        DUDE
. . . Also, my rug was stolen.

                    YOUNGER COP
Your rug was in the car?

The Dude taps the floor with his foot.

57

No. Here.

YOUNGER COP
Separate incidents?

The Dude stares at the floor.

Silence.

OLDER COP
. . . Snap out of it, son.

The home phone starts ringing – a ring distinct from the chirp of the portable. The Dude makes no move to answer it. Finally the rings stop as an answering machine kicks on.

DUDE
. . . You find them much? Stolen cars?

DUDE'S VOICE
(*on machine*)
The Dude's not in. Leave a message after the beep. It takes a minute.

YOUNGER COP
Sometimes. I wouldn't hold out much hope for the tape deck, though. Or the Creedence.

DUDE
And the, uh, the briefcase?

Beep.

FEMALE VOICE
Mr Lebowski, I'd like to see you. Call when you get home and I'll send a car for you. My name is Maude Lebowski. I'm the woman who took the rug.

Beep. Dial tone.

OLDER COP
Well, I guess we can close the file on that one.

LOFT

We are tracking forward through a large sparsely furnished downtown Los Angeles loft. A huge unfinished canvas, lit by standing industrial lights, dominates one wall. On the floor is the Dude's brilliant rug.

We hear a rumble like that of an approaching bowling ball. The Dude, his walk forward arrested, turns to peer into the murky space behind him.

Something huge and white hurtles toward the Dude's head. As it roars overhead he ducks, screaming, then spins to watch it pass.

The backside of a naked woman recedes. She is in a sling suspended from a ceiling track, and holds a paint bucket in one hand and brush in the other. As she rumbles over a canvas that lies on the floor she flicks paint down at it.

The Dude turns again as he hears running footsteps. Two young men in paint-spattered shorts, T-shirts and sneakers pursue the sling and catch up with it as it reaches the end of its track. They haul it back for another push.

VOICE

I'll be with you in a minute, Mr Lebowski.

The woman rumbles by in another pass.

. . . All right, we'll do the blue tomorrow. Elfranco. Pedro. Help me down.

The two men help Maude out of her sling. She is naked except for leather harness straps which ring her breasts and wrap her thighs and give her something of a dominatrix look.

. . . Does the female form make you uncomfortable, Mr Lebowski?

DUDE

Is that what that's a picture of?

MAUDE

In a sense, yes. Elfranco, my robe. My art has been commended as being strongly vaginal. Which bothers some

59

men. The word itself makes some men uncomfortable. Vagina.

> DUDE

Oh yeah?

> MAUDE

Yes, they don't like hearing it and find it difficult to say. Whereas without batting an eye a man will refer to his 'dick' or his 'rod' or his 'Johnson'.

> DUDE

'Johnson'?

> MAUDE

Thank you.

This to Elfranco, who has handed her a robe.

> . . . All right, Mr Lebowski, let's get down to cases. My father told me he's agreed to let you have the rug, but it was a gift from me to my late mother, and so was not his to give. Now. As for this . . . 'kidnapping' –

> DUDE

Huh?

> MAUDE

Yes, I know about it. And I know that you acted as courier. And let me tell you something: the whole thing stinks to high heaven.

> DUDE

Right, but let me explain something about that rug –

> MAUDE

Do you like sex, Mr Lebowski?

> DUDE

. . . Excuse me?

> MAUDE

Sex. The physical act of love. Coitus. Do you like it?

DUDE

I was talking about my rug.

MAUDE

You're not interested in sex?

DUDE

. . . You mean coitus?

MAUDE

I like it too. It's a male myth about feminists that we hate sex. It can be a natural, zesty enterprise. But unfortunately there are some people – it is called satyriasis in men, nymphomania in women – who engage in it compulsively and without joy.

DUDE

Oh, no.

MAUDE

Yes, Mr Lebowski, these unfortunate souls cannot love in the true sense of the word. Our mutual acquaintance Bunny is one of these.

DUDE

Listen, Maude, I'm sorry if your stepmother is a nympho, but I don't see what it has to do with – do you have any kalhua?

MAUDE

Take a look at this, sir.

She is aiming a remote at a projection TV.

The screen flickers to life.

Title cards:

JACKIE TREEHORN PRESENTS
KARL HUNGUS
and
BUNNY LAJOYA
in
LOGJAMMIN'

The Dude is at the bar, a bottle of kalhua frozen halfway to his glass.

From the television set we hear a doorbell ring, and then a door opening.

On the TV screen the door opens to reveal a sallow-faced man in blue cover-alls. It is Uli, the floater in Lebowski's pool.

ULI
Hello. Mein dizbatcher says zere iss problem mit deine kable.

DUDE
Shit, I know that guy. He's a nihilist.

MAUDE
And you recognize her, of course.

The girl answering the door is Bunny Lebowski.

BUNNY
The TV is in here.

ULI
Ja, okay. Ich bring mein toolz.

BUNNY
This is my friend Shari. She just came over to use the shower.

MAUDE
(*grimly*)
The story is ludicrous.

ULI
Mein nommen iss Karl. Is hard to verk in zese clozes . . .

MAUDE
Lord. You can imagine where it goes from here.

She switches off the set.

DUDE
. . . He fixes the cable?

MAUDE
Don't be fatuous, Jeffrey. Little matter to me that this woman chose to pursue a career in pornography, nor that she has

been 'banging' Jackie Treehorn, to use the parlance of our times. However. I am one of two trustees of the Lebowski Foundation, the other being my father. The Foundation takes youngsters from Watts and –

DUDE

Shit yeah, the achievers.

MAUDE

Little Lebowski Urban Achievers, yes, and proud we are of all of them. I asked my father about his withdrawal of a million dollars from the Foundation account and he told me about this 'abduction', but I tell you, it is preposterous. This compulsive fornicator is taking my father for the proverbial ride.

DUDE

Yeah, but my –

MAUDE

I'm getting to your rug. My father and I don't get along; he doesn't approve of my lifestyle and, needless to say, I don't approve of his. Still, I hardly wish to make my father's embezzlement a police matter, so I'm proposing that you try to recover the money from the people you delivered it to.

DUDE

Well – sure, I could do that –

MAUDE

If you successfully do so, I will compensate you to the tune of ten percent of the recovered sum.

DUDE

A hundred . . .

MAUDE

Thousand, yes, bones or clams or whatever you call them.

DUDE

Yeah, but what about –

MAUDE

– your rug, yes, well with that money you can buy any number of rugs that don't have sentimental value for *me*. And I *am* sorry about that crack on the jaw.

The Dude fingers his jaw, where the lump from the sap has all but disappeared.

DUDE

Oh, that's okay, I hardly even –

MAUDE

Here's the name and number of a doctor who will look at it for you. You will receive no bill. He's a good man, and thorough.

DUDE

That's really thoughtful but I –

MAUDE

Please see him, Jeffrey. He's a good man, and thorough.

A LIMO

The Dude rides in back holding a White Russian, listening to the chauffeur, a man of about the same age, from whose livery cap a ponytail emerges.

CHAUFFEUR

– So he says, 'My son can't hold a job, my daughter's married to a fuckin' loser, and I got a rash on my ass so bad I can't hardly siddown. But you know me. I can't complain.'

Through rasping laughter:

DUDE

Fuckin' A, man. I got a rash . . . Fuckin' A, man. I gotta tell ya, Tony . . .

A sip from his drink leaves milk on his mustache.

. . . I was feeling really shitty earlier in the day, I'd lost a little money, I was down in the dumps –

TONY

Aw, forget about it.

DUDE

Yeah, man! Fuck it! I can't be worrying about that shit. Life goes on!

The limo has rolled to a stop. The Dude gets out, still holding his drink.

TONY

Home sweet home, Mr L. Who's your friend in the Volkswagen?

DUDE

Huh?

His eyes on the rear-view mirror, Tony jerks a thumb over his shoulder.

TONY

He followed us here.

The Dude turns to look.

Halfway up the block a Volkswagen Bug has pulled over to the curb. In the driver's seat we see a fat man's shape.

The Dude scowls.

DUDE

When did he –

The Dude is grabbed from behind and muscled away in a half nelson by another uniformed chauffeur.

SECOND CHAUFFEUR

Into the limo, you sonofabitch. No arguments.

As he is frog-marched towards another limo the Dude holds his drink away from his chest and cups a hand underneath it.

DUDE

Fuck, man! There's a beverage here!

The waiting limo's back door is flung open.

INSIDE

The Dude is shoved in and the door is slammed behind him.

> LEBOWSKI
> Start talking and talk fast, you lousy bum!

> BRANDT
> We've been frantically trying to reach you, Dude.

Brandt and the Big Lebowski sit facing the Dude; Lebowski with a comforter across his knees.

> LEBOWSKI
> Where's my goddamn money, you bum?!

> DUDE
> Well we – I don't –

> LEBOWSKI
> They did not receive the money, you nitwit! They did not receive the goddamn money. HER LIFE WAS IN YOUR HANDS!

> BRANDT
> This is our concern, Dude.

> DUDE
> No, man, nothing is fucked here –

> LEBOWSKI
> NOTHING IS FUCKED?! THE GODDAMN PLANE HAS CRASHED INTO THE MOUNTAIN!

The Dude takes a hurried sip from his drink.

> DUDE
> C'mon man, who're you gonna believe? Those guys are – we dropped off the damn money –

> LEBOWSKI
> *We?!*

> DUDE
> I – the royal we, you know, the editorial – I dropped off the money, exactly as per – Look, I've got certain information, certain things have come to light, and uh, has it ever occurred

to you, man, that given the nature of all this new shit, that, uh, instead of running around blaming me, that this whole thing might just be, not, you know, not just such a simple, but uh – you know?

LEBOWSKI

What in God's holy name are you blathering about?

DUDE

I'll tell you what I'm blathering about! I got information – new shit has come to light and – shit, man! She kidnapped herself!

Lebowski stares at him, dumbstruck. His silence encourages the Dude:

... Well sure, look at it! Young trophy wife, I mean, in the parlance of our times, owes money all over town, including to known pornographers – and that's cool, that's cool – but I'm saying, she needs money, and of course they're gonna say they didn't get it 'cause she wants more, man, she's gotta feed the monkey, I mean – hasn't that ever occurred to you . . .? Sir?

LEBOWSKI
(*quietly*)

No. No Mr Lebowski, that had not occurred to me.

BRANDT

That had not occurred to us, Dude.

DUDE

Well, okay, you're not privy to all the new shit, so uh, you know, but that's what you pay me for. Speaking of which, would it be possible for me to get my twenty grand in cash? I gotta check this with my accountant of course, but my concern is that, you know, it could bump me into a higher tax –

LEBOWSKI

Brandt, give him the envelope.

DUDE

Well, okay, if you've already made out the check . . .

Brandt is handing him a letter-sized envelope which is distended by something inside.

We received it this morning . . .

The Dude, frowning, untucks its flap, takes out some cotton wadding and unrolls it.

LEBOWSKI

Since you have failed to achieve, even in the modest task that was your charge, since you have stolen my money, and since you have unrepentantly betrayed my trust . . .

The wadding, undone, reveals a smaller wad of taped-up gauze. The Dude undoes the tape with his fingernails and starts to unroll the inner package.

. . . I have no choice but to tell these bums that they should do whatever is necessary to recover their money from *you*, Jeffrey Lebowski. And with Brandt as my witness, I tell you this: Any further harm visited upon Bunny shall be visited tenfold upon *your* head.

Between thumb and forefinger the Dude holds up the contents of the package – a little toe, with emerald green nail polish.

. . . By God, sir. I will not abide another toe.

COFFEE SHOP

The Dude and Walter sit at the counter, both staring off into space, both absently clinking teaspoons in their coffee.

After a long beat:

WALTER

. . . That wasn't her toe.

DUDE

Whose toe was it, Walter?

WALTER

How the fuck should I know? I *do* know that nothing about it indicates –

DUDE

The nail polish, Walter.

WALTER

Fine, Dude. As if it's impossible to get some nail polish, apply it to someone else's toe –

DUDE

Someone else's – where the fuck are they gonna –

WALTER

You want a toe? I can get you a toe, believe me. There are ways, Dude. You don't wanna know about it, believe me.

DUDE

But, Walter –

WALTER

I'll get you a toe by three o'clock this afternoon – *with* nail polish. These fucking amateurs. They send us a toe, we're supposed to shit ourselves with fear. Jesus Christ. My point is –

DUDE

They're gonna kill her, Walter, and then they're gonna kill
me –

WALTER

Well that's just, that's the stress talking, Dude. So far we
have what looks to me like a series of victimless crimes –

DUDE

What about the toe?

WALTER

FORGET ABOUT THE FUCKING TOE!

A waitress enters.

WAITRESS

Could you please keep your voices down – this is a family
restaurant.

WALTER

Oh, please, dear! I've got news for you: the Supreme Court
has roundly *rejected* prior restraint!

DUDE

Walter, this isn't a First Amendment thing.

WAITRESS

Sir, if you don't calm down I'm going to have to ask you to
leave.

WALTER

Lady, I got buddies who died face down in the muck so you
and I could *enjoy* this family restaurant!

The Dude gets up.

DUDE

All right, I'm leaving. I'm sorry ma'am.

WALTER

Don't run away from this, Dude! Goddamnit, this affects all
of us!

The Dude has left frame; Walter calls after him:

... Our basic freedoms!

He looks around defiantly.

... I'm staying. Finishing my coffee.

He stirs the coffee, bopping his head in time to the muzak, affecting nonchalance.

... Finishing my coffee.

DUDE'S BATHROOM

A dripping noise.

The Dude sits in the bath-tub, staring stuporously, a joint pinched in one hand, a washcloth draped across his forehead.

He is staring at his toes splayed against the far side of the tub.

The phone is ringing in the other room. After the Dude's outgoing message we hear:

                    VOICE THROUGH MACHINE
    Mr Lebowski, this is Duty Officer Rolvaag of the LAPD ...

The Dude looks up hopefully, his head swaying.

    ... We've recovered your vehicle. It can be claimed at the
    North Hollywood Auto Circus there on Victory ...

                              DUDE
    Far out. Far fuckin' out.

                            MESSAGE
    You'll just need to present a –

The message is interrupted by loud smashing sounds, as of someone applying a baseball bat to the answering machine.

                              DUDE
    ... Hunh?

He looks blearily at the open doorway.

A tall man dressed in black leather with a cricket bat is striding across the living room toward the bathroom.

Hey! This is a private residence, man!

The man has entered the bathroom and, in stride, swings the cricket bat up to smash the overhead light. Two other men are entering behind him.

The room is dark now except for spill from the living room; the men are backlit shapes.

One of them holds a string at the other end of which a small animal skitters excitedly about the floor.

The Dude looks curiously at the small, nattering animal.

. . . Nice marmot.

The man with the string scoops up the marmot and tosses it, squealing, into the bath-tub.

The Dude screams.

The marmot splashes frantically, biting at the Dude in a frenzy of fearful aggression.

FIRST MAN
Vee vant zat money, Lebowski.

The Dude, screaming, grabs the lip of the tub and starts to hoist himself up but the first man lays a palm on top of his head and squushes him back into the water.

SECOND MAN
You think veer kidding und making mit de funny stuff?

THIRD MAN
Vee could do things you haffent dreamed of, Lebowski.

SECOND MAN
Ja, vee could really do it, Lebowski. Vee belief in nossing.

He scoops the marmot out of the water. It shakes itself off, spraying the Dude.

DUDE
Jesus!

ULI

Vee belief in nossing, Lebowski! NOSSING!

The marmot, back on the floor, skitters around shaking itself and convulsing with little sneezes.

DUDE

Jesus Christ!

FIRST MAN

Tomorrow vee come back und cut off your chonson.

DUDE

. . . Excuse me?

FIRST MAN

I SAY VEE CUT OFF YOUR CHONSON!

As the three men leave:

SECOND MAN

Just sink about zat, Lebowski.

FIRST MAN

Ja, your viggly penis, Lebowski.

SECOND MAN

Ja, und maybe vee stamp on it und skvush it, Lebowski . . .

NORTH HOLLYWOOD AUTO CIRCUS

A policeman with a clipboard is leading the Dude through a large parking lot.

POLICEMAN

She was discovered last night in Van Nuys, lodged against an abutment.

DUDE

Oh man – lodged where?!

POLICEMAN

You're lucky she wasn't chopped, Mr Lebowski. Must've been a joyride situation; they abandoned the car once they hit the retaining wall.

They have reached the Dude's car. The driver's side exterior has been scraped raw. The policeman hands the Dude a door handle and a side-view mirror.

. . . These were on the road next to the car. You'll have to get in on the other side.

The Dude climbs in the passenger side.

DUDE
My fucking briefcase! It's not here!

POLICEMAN
Yeah, sorry, I saw that on the report. You're lucky they left the tape deck though, and the Creedence.

DUDE
My fucking briefcase! My – Jesus! What's that smell?

POLICEMAN
Uh, yeah. Probably a vagrant, slept in the car. Or perhaps just used it as a toilet, and moved on.

The Dude tries to roll down the driver's window but it will not go; he bellows through the glass:

DUDE
When will you find these guys? I mean, do you have any promising leads?

The policeman laughs, agreeing broadly.

POLICEMAN
Leads, yeah. I'll just check with the boys down at the Crime Lab. They've assigned four more detectives to the case, got us working in shifts.

The Dude looks sadly through his window at the policeman, whose continuing laughter is muffled by the glass.

BOWLING ALLEY BAR

The Dude, Walter and Donny sit at the bar; the Dude with a White Russian, Walter with a beer and Donny eating beer nuts.

74

DONNY

. . . And then they're gonna *stamp* on it?!

WALTER

Oh, for Christ – will you shut the fuck up, Donny.

DUDE

I figure my only hope is that the Big Lebowski kills me before
the Germans can cut my dick off.

WALTER

Now that is ridiculous, Dude. No one is going to cut your
dick off.

DUDE

Thanks, Walter.

WALTER

Not if I have anything to say about it.

DUDE

Yeah, thanks, Walter. That gives me a very secure feeling.

WALTER

Dude –

DUDE

That makes me feel all warm inside.

WALTER

Now, Dude –

DUDE

This whole fucking thing – I *could* be sitting here with just
pee-stains on my rug.

Walter sadly shakes his head.

WALTER

Fucking Germans. Nothing changes. Fucking Nazis.

DONNY

They were Nazis, Dude?

WALTER

Come on, Donny, they were threatening castration!

DONNY

Uh-huh.

WALTER

Are you gonna split hairs?

DONNY

No –

WALTER

Am I wrong?

DONNY

Well –

DUDE

They're nihilists.

WALTER

Huh?

DUDE

They kept saying they believe in nothing.

WALTER

Nihilists! Jesus . . .

Walter looks haunted.

. . . Say what you like about the tenets of National Socialism, Dude, at least it's an ethos.

DUDE

Yeah.

WALTER

And let's also not forget – let's not forget, Dude – that keeping wildlife, an amphibious rodent, for uh, domestic, you know, within the city – *that* isn't legal either.

DUDE

What're you, a fucking park ranger now?

WALTER

No, I'm –

DUDE

Who gives a shit about the fucking marmot!

WALTER

– We're sympathizing here, Dude –

DUDE

Fuck your sympathy! I don't need your sympathy, man, I
need my fucking Johnson!

DONNY

What do you need that for, Dude?

WALTER

You gotta buck up, man. You can't go into the tournament
with this negative attitude –

DUDE

Fuck the tournament! Fuck you, Walter!

There is a moment of stunned silence.

WALTER

. . . Fuck the tournament?!
(*sad; quiet*)
. . . Okay, Dude. I can see you don't want to be cheered up.
C'mon, Donny, let's go get a lane.

*They leave the Dude sitting morosely at the bar. As he stares down
into his empty glass:*

DUDE

Another Caucasian, Gary.

VOICE

Right, Dude.

DUDE

Friends like these, huh, Gary.

GARY

That's right, Dude.

The pop song on the jukebox has ended; someone puts on 'Tumbling Tumbleweeds'.

A man saunters up to the bar to take the stool next to the Dude's. He is middle-aged and craggily handsome – Sam Elliott, perhaps. He has a large Western-style mustache and wears denims, a yoked shirt and a cowboy hat.

MAN
(*to the bartender*)

D'ya have a good sarsaparilla?

We recognize the voice of The Stranger whose narration opened the movie.

BARTENDER

Sioux City Sarsaparilla.

The stranger nods.

THE STRANGER

That's a good'un.

Waiting for his drink, he looks amiably around the bar. His crinkled eyes settle on the Dude.

. . . How ya doin' there, Dude?

The Dude, still staring down at his drink, shakes his head.

DUDE

Ahh, not so good, man.

THE STRANGER

One a those days, huh? Wal, a wiser fella than m'self once said, sometimes you eat the bar and sometimes the bar, wal, he eats you.

DUDE
(*absently*)

Uh-huh. That some kind of Eastern thing?

THE STRANGER
Far from it.

The bartender puts a brown bottle and a frosted glass on the bar in front of The Stranger, who touches his hat brim.

. . . Much obliged.

He looks back at the Dude.

. . . I like your style, Dude.

The Dude looks up and notices The Stranger for the first time.

DUDE
. . . Well, I like your style too, man. Got a whole cowboy thing goin'.

THE STRANGER
Thankie . . . Just one thing, Dude. D'ya *have* to use s'many cuss words?

DUDE
. . . The fuck are you talking about?

The Stranger chuckles indulgently and pushes off from the bar.

THE STRANGER
Okay, have it your way.

He brushes his hat brim with a fingertip.

. . . Taker easy, Dude.

DUDE
Yeah . . . thanks man.

He is gone. 'Tumbling Tumbleweeds' is just fading away as – BANG – a telephone is slapped down onto the bar in front of the Dude. He looks at it.

BARTENDER
(off-screen)
Call for ya, Dude.

The Dude picks up the handset.

80

DUDE

... Hello?

MAUDE
(*from phone*)
Jeffrey, you have not gone to the doctor.

DUDE

Huh? Oh, yeah, no, I uh –

MAUDE
(*from phone*)
I'd like to see you immediately.

DUDE

Oh . . .

ELEVATOR DOOR

It slides open at the cut to reveal Maude's loft. Sitting on the sofa is a tall man with dark slicked-back hair, wearing a light-colored Italian suit. His long legs are casually crossed and he is looking up from a copy of Architectural Digest.

MAN

You're Lebowski?

The man takes in the Dude's bowling attire and shades with an amused grin.

DUDE

Yeah.

MAN

Ha-ha-ha-ha. Maudie told me about you. Go ahead, sit down. She'll be back in a minute. Want a drink?

DUDE

Sure. White Russian?

The man gives a nonchalant wave of the head:

MAN

Bar's over there.

DUDE

Uh. Yeah.

The man still watches him with an amused smile.

MAN

What do you do, Lebowski?

DUDE

Hey, who the fuck are you, man?

MAN

Friend of Maudie's.

DUDE

Oh yeah? The friend with the cleft asshole?

MAN

Ha-ha-ha-ha.

DUDE

What do *you* do?

MAN

Oh, nothing much.

Still smiling, he goes back to his magazine.

The elevator is opening again and Maude emerges.

MAUDE

Hello, Jeffrey.

DUDE

Yeah, how are ya?

She has crossed to the man, John, on the sofa with whom she exchanges a kiss of greeting.

DUDE

Listen, Maude, I gotta respectfully, you know, tender my resignation or whatever, 'cause it looks like your mother really was kidnapped after all.

MAUDE

She most certainly was not!

83

DUDE

Hey man, why don't you fucking listen occasionally? You might learn something. Now I got –

MAUDE

And please don't call her my mother.

JOHN

Ha-ha-ha-ha.

DUDE

Now I got –

MAUDE

She is most definitely the perpetrator and not the victim.

DUDE

I'm telling you, I got pretty definitive evidence –

MAUDE

From who?

DUDE

The main guy, Uli –

MAUDE

Uli Kunkle?

DUDE

Well – yeah, I guess –

MAUDE

Her 'co-star' in the beaver picture?

DUDE

Beaver? You mean vagina? – I mean, you know him?

MAUDE

I might even have introduced them, for all I know. You remember Uli?

This last to John who, still smiling down at the magazine, nods.

JOHN

Mm.

MAUDE

... He's a ... musician, used to have a group – 'Autobahn'
– look in my LPs – they released one album in the late
seventies ...

*The Dude fingers through the albums filling one bookshelf. He stops
between two albums.*

DUDE

Roy Orbison ... Pink Floyd.

MAUDE

Huh? *Auto*bahn. *A-u*-t-o. Their music is a sort of – ugh –
techno-pop ...

*The Dude pulls out an album with a worn sleeve. On it is the group's
name,* Autobahn, *the album name,* Nagelbett, *and a picture of three
young Germans, their foreheads looming below slicked-back hair,
gazing upward in thin-lipped epiphany. They are wearing severe but
modishly retro suits. Each has his name under his picture – Uli, Kieffer
and Franz. A bed of nails is the cyc's only set dressing.*

... Believe me, he's not the brains behind the operation, or
behind anything. So he's pretending to be the abductor?

DUDE

Well ... yeah –

MAUDE

Look, Jeffrey, you don't *really* kidnap someone that you're
acquainted with. The whole idea is that the hostage can't
be able to identify you after you've let them go.

DUDE

Well yeah ... *I* know that ...

The sniggering John is still leafing through the magazine:

JOHN

Ha-ha-ha-ha.

DUDE

Hey, what the fuck is with this guy? Who is he?

Maude looks at the Dude as if he must be exceptionally dense.

85

MAUDE

John *Harrington*. The video artist.

JOHN

Ha-ha-ha-ha.

MAUDE

So Uli has the money?

DUDE

Well, no, not exactly. It's a complicated case, Maude. Lotta ins. Lotta outs. Lotta what-have-yous. And a lotta strands to keep in my head, man.

The phone rings. John Harrington reaches over to answer it.

. . . Lotta strands in ol' Duder's head.

MAUDE

Well if Uli doesn't have it, who –

JOHN

Si si, arriviamo al quindici –

(to Maude)
– It's Sandro, calling about the *Biennale* –
(back into the phone)
. . . *e speriamo di rivederte* . . .

As John prattles on in Italian, Maude turns back to the Dude.

MAUDE
Look, I have to take this – Do you still have that doctor's
number?

DUDE
Huh? No, really, I don't even have the bruise any more,
I –

Maude is scribbling.

MAUDE
Please, Jeffrey. I don't want to be responsible for any delayed
after-effects.

DUDE
Delayed after-eff –

I want you to see him immediately. This is his address. He assured me he'd take you without appointment. He's a good man, and thorough.

She is picking up an extension. Finished with the Dude, she speaks to her friend in fluent Italian. She titters; John starts laughing; he laughs harder; she laughs harder.

The Dude looks from one to the other, both now roaring with laughter.

CLOSE SHOT: THE DUDE

His eyes are closed, a headset on, his shirt off. Music leaks tinnily through his headset.

Behind him, cropped so that we see only a little of his torso, a white-smocked figure taps at the Dude's back.

After a moment the figure circles to one side, out of frame. His hand reaches in to pull one arm of the headset away from the Dude's ear, and as he does so the music issues more strongly.

VOICE
Could you slide your shorts down please, Mr Lebowski?

The Dude's eyes open.

DUDE
Huh? No, she, she hit me right here.

VOICE
I understand, sir. Could you slide your shorts down, please?

DUDE'S CAR

The Dude is driving home. A Creedence tape plays.

The Dude is sucking down a joint. He glances at the rear-view mirror – and, noticing something, looks again.

A Volkswagen Bug is following, a lone fat man driving.

The Dude, his eyes still on the mirror, absently takes the joint between thumb and forefinger of his right hand and flicks it out the driver's window – except that the window is not open. The butt bounces off the glass and around the car, showering sparks.

It settles, glowing, in the Dude's crotch.

The Dude screams.

THE STREET

The car careens wildly and the surrounding traffic veers off to make way, horns blaring. The car finally spins and comes to rest with its passenger side wrapped into a telephone poll.

INSIDE THE CAR

The Dude frantically grabs at his door, which won't open, and then slides over to push at the passenger door, which also won't open.

DUDE

Fuck Marie . . .

Sitting on the passenger side now, he looks around for the burning roach.

Smoke wisps up from between the driver's seat cushion and back cushion.

. . . Fuckola, man . . .

He takes his beer and pours it in between the cushions.

The corner of a piece of paper sticks out from between the cushions.

The Dude pulls it out.

It is lined spiral notebook paper, slightly singed and dripping beer, covered with handwriting. In the upper right-hand corner is the name 'Lawrence Sellers', and under that, 'Mrs Jamtoss, 5th Period'. The theme is titled 'The Louisiana Purchase'. In red ink is a large circled D and some handwritten marginal comments; misspelled words are circled in red throughout.

We are behind Walter, the Dude and Donny, facing the stage in the background where Marty, the Dude's balding landlord, is performing a danse moderne.

Walter leans in to talk to the Dude in a hushed voice so as not to disturb what little there is of audience.

WALTER

He lives in North Hollywood on Radford, near the In-and-Out Burger –

DUDE

The In-and-Out Burger is on Camrose.

WALTER

Near the In-and-Out Burger –

DONNY

Those are good burgers, Walter.

WALTER

Shut the fuck up, Donny. This kid is in the ninth grade, Dude, and his father is – are you ready for this? – Arthur Digby Sellers.

DUDE

Who the fuck is that?

WALTER

Huh?

DUDE

Who the fuck is Arthur Digby Sellers?

WALTER

Who the f – have you ever heard of a little show called *Branded*, Dude?

DUDE

Yeah.

WALTER

All but one man died? There at Bitter Creek?

90

DUDE

Yeah yeah, I know the fucking show Walter, so what?

WALTER

Fucking Arthur Digby Sellers wrote 156 episodes, Dude.

DUDE

Uh-huh.

WALTER

The bulk of the series.

DUDE

Uh-huh.

WALTER

Not exactly a lightweight.

DUDE

No.

WALTER

And yet his son is a fucking dunce.

DUDE

Uh.

WALTER

Yeah, go figure. Well we'll go out there after the, uh, the . . .

He waves a hand vaguely toward the stage.

. . . what have you. We'll, uh –

DONNY

We'll be near the In-and-Out Burger.

WALTER

Shut the fuck up, Donny. We'll, uh, brace the kid – he'll be a pushover. We'll get that fucking money, if he hasn't spent it already. Million fucking clams. And yes, we'll be near the, uh – some burgers, some beers, a few laughs. Our fucking troubles are over, Dude.

RESIDENTIAL AREA

The Dude and Walter are pulling up in front of a dilapidated house sitting on a scrubby lot. Parked incongruously before the house is a brand-new red Corvette.

DUDE
Fuck me, man! That kid's already spent all the money!

WALTER
Hardly, Dude, a new 'vette? The kid's still got, oh, 960 to 970 thousand, depending on the options. Wait in the car, Donny.

THE FRONT DOOR

Walter rings the bell. It is opened by a matronly Spanish woman.

WOMAN
Jace?

WALTER
Hello, Pilar? My name is Walter Sobchak. We spoke on the phone, this is my associate Jeffrey Lebowski.

WOMAN
Jace?

WALTER
May we, uh, we wanted to talk about little Larry. May we come in?

WOMAN
Jace?

They enter a dim living room and stand, looking about, as Pilar calls up the stairs:

PILAR
Larry! Sweetie! Dat mang is here!

There is a rhythmic compressor sound; Walter places it and nudges the Dude. At the other end of the living room a man lies on something that looks like a hospital gurney enclosed by a steel bubble.

It is an iron lung, breathing artificially with distinct hisses in and out.

> WALTER
> (sotto voce)
>
> That's him, Dude.
> (viva voce)
> . . . And a good day to you, sir.

> PILAR
>
> See down, please.

> WALTER
>
> Thank you, ma'am.

He and the Dude sit on a sagging green sofa.

> (in a lowered voice; to Pilar)
> . . . Does he, uh . . . Is he still writing?

> PILAR
>
> No, no. He has healt' problems.

> WALTER
>
> Uh-huh.

He bellows across the room:

> . . . I just want to say, sir, that we're both enormous – on a personal level, *Branded*, especially the early episodes, has been a source of, uh, inspir –

There are footsteps on the stairs. Larry, a fifteen-year-old, looks at the two men.

> PILAR
>
> See down, sweetie. These are the policeman –

> WALTER
>
> No ma'am, I didn't mean to give the impression that we're police exactly. We're hoping that it will not be necessary to call the police.

In turning to Larry he adopts his command voice:

> . . . But that is up to little Larry here. Isn't it, Larry?

Walter pops the latches on his attaché case and takes out the homework, which is now in a Ziploc bag. He shows it to Little Larry.

. . . Is this your homework, Larry?

Little Larry does not respond.

. . . Is this your homework, Larry?

DUDE

Look, man, did you –

WALTER

Dude, please . . . Is this your homework, Larry?

DUDE

Just ask him if he – ask him about the car, man!

Walter is still holding out the homework.

WALTER

Is this yours, Larry? Is this your homework, Larry?

DUDE

Is the car out front yours?

WALTER

Is this your homework, Larry?

DUDE

We know it's his fucking homework, Walter!
Where's the fucking money, you little brat?

WALTER

Look, Larry . . . Have you ever heard of Vietnam?

DUDE

Oh, for Christ's sake, Walter –

WALTER

You're going to enter a world of pain, son. We know that
this is your homework. We know you stole a car –

DUDE

And the fucking money!

And the fucking money. And we know that this is your
homework, Larry.

No answer.

. . . You're KILLING your FATHER, Larry! . . .

Finally, in disgust:

. . . Ah, this is pointless.

As he shoves the homework back in the attaché case:

. . . All right, Plan B. You might want to watch out the front
window there, Larry.

He is heading for the door. The Dude, puzzled, rises to follow.

. . . This is what happens when you FUCK a STRANGER in the
ASS, Larry.

OUTSIDE

*Walter is striding down the lawn with his attaché case, like an enraged
encyclopedia salesman.*

WALTER
Fucking language problem.

*He pops the Dude's trunk, flings in the briefcase and takes out a tire
iron.*

. . . Maybe he'll understand this.

He is walking over to the Corvette.

. . . YOU SEE WHAT HAPPENS, LARRY!

CRASH! He swings the crowbar into the windshield, which shatters.

. . . YOU SEE WHAT HAPPENS?!

CRASH! He takes out the driver's window.

. . . THIS IS WHAT HAPPENS WHEN YOU FUCK A STRANGER IN THE
ASS!

95

Lights are going on in houses down the street. Distant dogs bark.

    . . . HERE'S WHAT HAPPENS, LARRY!

CRASH!

    . . . HERE'S WHAT HAPPENS! FUCK A STRANGER IN THE ASS!

CRASH!

A man in a sleeveless T-shirt and boxer shorts has run over and grabs the crowbar from behind on its backswing.

MAN

WHAT THE FUCK JOO DOING, MANG?!

He wrestles the crowbar away from the startled Walter.

    . . . HIGH CHESS BAW DEECE FUCKEEN CAR LASS WEEK!

Walter cringes before the enraged Mexican.

WALTER

  . . . Hunh?

The man looks about wildly.

MAN

I KILL JOO, MANG! I – I KILL JOR FUCKEEN CAR!

He runs over to the Dude's car.

DUDE

No! No! NO! *THAT'S NOT –*

CRASH! CRASH!

MAN

I FUCKEEN KILL JOR FUCKEEN CAR!

CRASH!

    . . . I KILL JOR FUCKEEN CAR!

CRASH!

    . . . I KILL JOR FUCKEEN CAR!

THE DUDE'S CAR

We are looking in through the broken windshield as the car rattles down the freeway. Wind whistles through its caved-in windows.

The Dude drives, his jaw clenched, staring grimly out at the road. Walter, beside him, and Donny in the back seat, munch In-and-Out Burgers.

DUDE'S BUNGALOW

As he talks on the phone the Dude is hammering a two-by-four into the floor just inside, and parallel to, the front door.

> DUDE
> ... I accept your apology ... No I, I just want to handle it myself from now on ... No ... That has nothing to do with it ... Yes, it made it home, you're *calling* me at home ... No, Walter, it *didn't* look like Larry was about to crack ...

He finishes hammering, rises and grabs a straight-backed chair that stands nearby.

> ... Well that's your perception ... Well you're right, Walter, and the unspoken message is FUCK YOU AND LEAVE ME THE FUCK ALONE ... Yeah, I'll be at practice.

He hangs up and has just finished sliding the chair into place with its top under the doorknob and its legs braced against the two-by-four, thus wedging the door closed, when the door is opened – outwards. The chair clatters to the floor.

Woo and the blond man – the two rug vandals – stride in, kicking the chair away.

> WOO
> Pin your diapers on, Lebowski. Jackie Treehorn wants to see you.

> BLOND MAN
> And we know which Lebowski *you* are, Lebowski.

Yeah. Jackie Treehorn wants to talk to the deadbeat
Lebowski.

BLOND MAN
You're not dealing with morons here.

BLACKNESS

*Out of the blackness something is falling toward us. It is a woman,
falling in slow motion, limbs flailing. She is topless. She falls past the
camera, leaving blackness, then after a beat reappears, rising into
the night sky.*

*A crowd of mostly tanned middle-aged men with blow-dried hair,
wearing jogging outfits and other expensively casual attire, are
blanket-tossing the squealing young woman in nightmarish slow
motion.*

*It is a party, lit by festive beach lights and standing kerosene heaters.
1960s mainstream jazz, of the Mancini–Brubeck school, has been
piped down to speakers on the beach.*

*In long shot now the woman rises, squealing, disappears into darkness,
descends into light, rises again.*

*A man walks toward the camera through the pools of beach light. He
is handsome, fiftyish, wearing cotton twill pants and an expensively
casual shirt with a foulard knotted at the neck. Behind him, the
woman rises and falls, appears and disappears.*

MAN
Hello, Dude, thanks for coming. I'm Jackie Treehorn.

INSIDE THE BEACH HOUSE

The Dude is looking around at the sixties modern decor.

DUDE
This is quite a pad you got here, man. Completely unspoiled.

TREEHORN
What's your drink, Dude?

DUDE

White Russian, thanks. How's the smut business, Jackie?

TREEHORN

I wouldn't know, Dude. I deal in publishing, entertainment, political advocacy, and –

DUDE

Which one was *Logjammin'*?

TREEHORN

Regrettably, it's true, standards have fallen in adult entertainment. It's video, Dude. Now that we're competing with the amateurs, we can't afford to invest that little extra in story, production value, feeling . . .

He taps his forehead with one finger.

. . . People forget that the brain is the biggest erogenous zone.

DUDE

On you, maybe.

Treehorn hands him his drink.

TREEHORN

Of course, you do get the good with the bad. The new technology permits us to do exciting things with interactive erotic software. Wave of the future, Dude. Hundred percent electronic.

DUDE

Uh-huh. Well, I still jerk off manually.

TREEHORN

Of course you do. I can see you're anxious for me to get to the point. Well, Dude, here it is. Where's Bunny?

DUDE

I thought you might know, man.

TREEHORN

Me? How would I know? The only reason she ran off was to get away from her rather sizeable debt to me.

99

DUDE

But she hasn't run off, she's been –

Treehorn waves this off:

TREEHORN

I've heard the kidnapping story, so save it. I know you're
mixed up in all this, Dude, and I don't care what you're
trying to take off her husband. That's your business. All I'm
saying is, I want mine.

DUDE

Yeah, well, right man, there are many facets to this, uh, you
know, many interested parties. If I *can* find your money,
man – what's in it for the Dude?

TREEHORN

Of course, there's that to discuss. Refill?

DUDE

Does the Pope shit in the woods?

TREEHORN

Let's say a ten percent finder's fee?

DUDE

Okay, Jackie, done. I like the way you do business. Your
money is being held by a kid named Larry Sellers. He lives
in North Hollywood, on Radford, near the In-and-Out
Burger. A real fuckin' brat, but I'm sure your goons'll be able
to get it off him, I mean he's only fifteen and he's flunking
social studies. So if you'll just write me a check for my ten
percent . . . of a million . . . fifty grand . . .

He is getting to his feet, but sways woozily.

. . . I'll go out and mingle – Jesus, you mix a hell of a
Caucasian, Jackie.

The Dude shakes his head, trying to clear it.

TREEHORN

A fifteen-year-old? Is this your idea of a joke?

Jackie Treehorn's image starts to swim. He is joined on either side by Woo and the blond man.

DUDE

No funny stuff, Jackie . . . the kid's got it . . . Hiya, fellas . . . kid just wanted a car . . . all the Dude ever wanted . . . was his rug back . . . not greedy . . . it really . . .

He squints up at Jackie Treehorn, trying to keep him in focus.

. . . tied the room together.

He tips forward, spilling his drink off the table.

We look up from under the glass coffee table as the Dude's face drops toward us, hits the glass, and squushes.

FAST FADE OUT

BLACK

THE STRANGER'S VOICE

Darkness warshed over the Dude – darker'n a black steer's tookus on a moonless prairie night. There was no bottom.

We hear a thrumming bass.

TITLE CARDS:

JACKIE TREEHORN PRESENTS

THE DUDE

and

MAUDE LEBOWSKI

in

GUTTERBALLS

The title logo is a suggestively upright bowling pin flanked by a pair of bowling balls. The bending bass turns into the lead-in to Kenny Rogers and the First Edition's 'Just Dropped In'.

The Dude is walking down a long corridor dressed as a cable repairman. The corridor opens onto a gleaming bowling alley.

In the center of the alley stands Maude Lebowski, singing operatic harmony to the Kenny Rogers song. She wears an armored breastplate and bicorneal Norse headgear, has braided pigtails, and holds a trident.

The Dude presses up against her from behind to help with her follow-through as she releases a bowling ball.

The lane is now straddled by a line of chorines with arms akimbo Busby Berkeley-style, their legs turning the lane into a tunnel that leads to the pins at the end.

But it is no longer a bowling ball rolling between their legs – it is the Dude himself, levitating inches off the lane, the tools from his utility belt swinging free. He is face down, his arms, torpedo-like, pressed against his sides.

His point of view shows the lane rushing by below, the little ball-guide arrows zipping by.

The Dude twists into a barrel-roll so that he is now gliding along the lane face-up.

He looks up the dresses of the passing chorines.

The Dude smiles dreamily and does a backstroke motion to initiate another barrel-roll so that he is once again gliding face down. As he looks ahead, his forward momentum blows back his hair.

Coming at us, as we go through the last few pairs of legs, are the approaching pins. We hit the pins, scattering them, and rush on into black.

A body drops down into the blackness in slow motion – a topless woman, squealing, her legs kicking.

After she drops out of frame to leave us in black again, three men emerge in the background, entering a pool of toplight. It is the Germans, advancing ominously, wielding oversized shears which they scissor menacingly.

The Dude, now standing in a field of black, reacts to the advancing Germans. He turns and runs, fists pumping.

The scissoring sound of the shears turns into the whoosh of passing cars. The field of black is punctured by headlights. The Dude is running blearily down the middle of the Pacific Coast Highway. Cars rush by on either side, horns blaring.

With the BLOO-WHUP *of a tap on its siren, a squad car pulls up, its gumballs flashing.*

SQUAD CAR

The Dude sits in the back seat, his head lolling with the motion of the car as he slurs the theme of Branded:

> DUDE
>
> He was innocent . . .
> Not a charge was true . . .
> And they say he ran awaaaaaay . . .

CHIEF'S OFFICE

The Dude is hurled against and bounces off the Chief's desk. He comes to rest more or less seated in a facing chair.

His wallet is tossed onto the desk.

The Chief leans forward, takes the wallet, and sorts through it with the weary disdain of a cop who has seen it all and not cared for any of it.

He looks at the Ralph's Shopper's Club card.

> CHIEF
>
> This is your only ID?

> DUDE
>
> I know my rights.

> CHIEF
>
> You don't know shit, Lebowski.

> DUDE
>
> I want a fucking lawyer, man. I want Bill Kunstler.

> CHIEF
>
> What are you, some kind of sad-assed refugee from the fucking sixties?

> DUDE
>
> Uh-huh.

CHIEF

Mr Treehorn tells us that he had to eject you from his garden party, that you were drunk and abusive.

DUDE

That guy treats women like objects, man.

CHIEF

Mr Treehorn draws a lot of water in this town, Lebowski. You don't draw shit. We got a nice quiet beach community here, and I aim to keep it nice and quiet. So let me make something plain. I don't like you sucking around bothering our citizens, Lebowski. I don't like your jerk-off name, I don't like your jerk-off face, I don't like your jerk-off behavior, and I don't like *you*, jerk-off – Do I make myself clear?

The Dude stares.

DUDE

. . . I'm sorry, I wasn't listening.

The Chief hurls his mug of steaming coffee at the Dude. It clanks against his forehead and sends scalding coffee everywhere.

Ow! Fucking fascist!

The Chief is up off his chair, rounding the desk.

CHIEF

Stay out of Malibu, Lebowski!

He slaps the Dude, kicks the chair out from under him, and then starts kicking at the Dude himself.

. . . Stay out of Malibu, deadbeat! Keep your ugly fucking goldbricking ass out of my beach community!

CAB

The Dude, in the back seat of a taxi-cab that rocks and squeaks with every seam in the road, is gingerly touching at sore spots on his face and scalp.

'Peaceful Easy Feeling' is on the radio.

                          DUDE
Jesus, man, can you change the station?

                         DRIVER
Fuck you, man! You don't like my fucking music, get your
own fucking cab!

                          DUDE
I've had a –

                         DRIVER
I pull over and kick your ass out, man!

                          DUDE
– had a rough night, and I hate the fucking Eagles, man –

                         DRIVER
That's it! Outa this fucking cab!

THE STREET

The cab screeches to the curb.

*As the driver hops out and hauls the Dude from the back seat, another
car speeds by, its radio blaring.*

INSIDE THE OTHER CAR

*It is a red convertible. The driver, singing loudly and badly along with
the radio, her hair blowing in the wind, is Bunny Lebowski.*

THE FOOTWELL

*Her right foot rests on the accelerator in an open-toed, bright red high-
heeled shoe, showing five painted toes.*

When she downshifts, her left foot enters to engage the clutch.

Five more toes.

DUDE'S BUNGALOW

*The Dude staggers in the open front door and looks around, one hand
pressed to a lump on his forehead.*

DUDE

... Jesus.

The place is a wreck. Furniture has been overturned, upholstery slashed, drawers dumped.

Quiet.

The door to the bedroom creaks open.

The Dude cringes.

Maude emerges from the bedroom. She is wearing a bathrobe.

MAUDE

Jeffrey.

DUDE

... Maude?

She pulls open the bathrobe as she approaches.

MAUDE

Love me.

The Dude is puzzled.

DUDE

... That's my robe.

THOOMP! *On their embrace we cut to:*

BLACK

After a beat, a long sigh, and then a voice from the blackness:

MAUDE

... Tell me a little about yourself, Jeffrey.

DUDE

Well, uh ... Not much to tell ...

A match is dragged across a headboard; the Dude is lighting himself a joint.

... I was, uh, one of the authors of the Port Huron Statement – The *original* Port Huron Statement.

MAUDE

Uh-huh.

DUDE

Not the compromised second draft. And then I, uh . . . Ever
hear of the Seattle Seven?

MAUDE

Mmnun.

DUDE

Mm. And then . . . let's see, I uh – music business briefly.

MAUDE

Oh?

DUDE

Yeah. Roadie for Metallica. Speed of Sound Tour.

MAUDE

Uh-huh.

DUDE

Bunch of assholes. And then, you know, little of this, little
of that. My career's, uh, slowed down a bit lately.

MAUDE

What do you do for fun?

DUDE

Oh, you know, the usual. Bowl. Drive around. The
occasional acid flashback.

*He climbs out of bed. Maude spreads out, wedges a pillow into the
small of her back and clasps a hand on each kneecap. She pulls her
knees in toward her chest to keep her pelvis raised.*

MAUDE

. . . What happened to your house?

DUDE

Jackie Treehorn trashed the place. Wanted to save the
finder's fee.

MAUDE

Finder's fee?

DUDE

He thought I had your father's money, so he got me out of the way while he looked for it.

MAUDE

It's not my father's money, it's the Foundation's. Why did he think *you* had it? And who does?

DUDE

Larry Sellers, a high-school kid. Real fucking brat.

He picks a White Russian off the bedside table.

MAUDE

Jeffrey –

DUDE

It's a complicated case, Maude. Lotta ins, lotta outs. Fortunately I've been adhering to a pretty strict, uh, drug regimen to keep my mind, you know, limber. I'm real fucking close to your father's money, real fucking close. It's just –

MAUDE

I keep telling you, it's the *Foundation's* money. Father doesn't have any.

DUDE

. . . Huh? He's fucking loaded.

MAUDE

No no, the wealth was all Mother's.

DUDE

But your father – he runs stuff, he –

MAUDE

We did let Father run one of the companies, briefly, but he didn't do very well at it.

DUDE

But he's –

MAUDE

He helps administer the charities now, and I give him a
reasonable allowance. He has no money of his own. I know
how he likes to present himself; Father's weakness is vanity.
Hence the slut.

DUDE

Huh. Jeez. Well, so, did he – is that yoga?

*Throughout, Maude has been lying on her back with her knees
pulled in.*

MAUDE

It increases the chances of conception.

The Dude spits some White Russian.

DUDE

*In*creases?

MAUDE

Well yes, what did you think this was all about? Fun and
games?

DUDE

Well . . . no, of course not –

MAUDE

I want a child.

DUDE

Yeah, okay, but see, the Dude –

MAUDE

Look, Jeffrey, I don't want a partner. In fact I don't want
the father to be someone I have to see socially, or who'll
have any interest in rearing the child himself.

DUDE

Huh . . .

Something occurs to him.

. . . So . . . that doctor . . .

Exactly. What happened to your face? Did Jackie Treehorn
do that as well?

The Dude is staring off into space, thinking. His reply is absent:

DUDE
No, the, uh, chief of police of Malibu. A real reactionary . . .
So your father . . . Oh man, I get it!

MAUDE
What?

The Dude is leaving the bedroom.

DUDE
Yeah, my thinking about the case, man, it had become
uptight. Yeah. Your father –

LIVING ROOM

The Dude finishes punching a number into the phone.

PHONE VOICE
This is Walter Sobchak. I'm not in; leave a message after the
beep.

From the bedroom:

MAUDE'S VOICE
What're you talking about?

Beep.

DUDE
Walter, if you're there, pick up the fucking phone. Pick it
up, Walter, this is an emergency. I'm not –

WALTER
Dude?

DUDE
Walter, listen, I'm at my place, I need you to come pick me
up –

WALTER

I can't drive, Dude, it's erev shabbas.

DUDE

Huh?

WALTER

Erev shabbas. I can't drive. I'm not even supposed to pick
up the phone unless it's an emergency.

DUDE

It *is* a fucking emergency.

WALTER

I understand. That's why I picked up the phone.

DUDE

THEN WHY CAN'T YOU – fuck, never mind, just call Donny
then, and ask him to –

WALTER

Dude, I'm not supposed to make calls –

DUDE

WALTER, YOU FUCKING ASSHOLE, WE GOTTA GO TO PASADENA!
COME PICK ME UP OR I'M OFF THE FUCKING BOWLING TEAM!

MAUDE'S VOICE

Jeffrey?

THE DUDE

He emerges on his front stoop, pulling on a shirt.

His attention is caught by something down the street.

*A car is parked halfway down the block. We can see the silhouette of
a fat man in the driver's seat.*

The Dude starts down the street toward the car.

*The fat man leans forward and we hear the sound of the car's starter
coughing. The engine will not turn over. More whines and coughs;
no ignition.*

The man hurriedly fumbles to one side and brings up a newspaper, which he holds before his face.

The Dude gets to the car, reaches through the open driver's window and grabs the newspaper and hurls it to the ground.

> DUDE
>
> Get out of that fucking car, man!

The man nervously complies. The Dude flinches at the man's movement as he gets out. The man cringes in turn, reacting to the Dude's flinch.

He is wearing a cheap blue serge suit. He is bald with a short fringe and a mustache.

The Dude shouts to cover his fear:

> Who the fuck are you, man! Come on, man!

> MAN
>
> Relax, man! No physical harm intended!

> DUDE
>
> Who the fuck are you? Why've you been following me? Come on, fuckhead!

> MAN
>
> Hey, relax man, I'm a brother shamus.

The Dude is stunned.

> DUDE
>
> . . . Brother Seamus? Like an Irish monk?

> MAN
>
> Irish m – What the fuck are you talking about? My name's Da Fino! I'm a private snoop! Like you, man!

> DUDE
>
> Huh?

> DA FINO
>
> A dick, man! And let me tell you something: I dig your work. Playing one side against the other – in bed with everybody – fabulous stuff, man.

DUDE

I'm not a – ah, fuck it, just stay away from my fucking lady
friend, man.

DA FINO

Hey hey, I'm not messing with your special lady –

DUDE

She's not my special lady, she's my fucking lady friend. I'm
just helping her conceive, man!

DA FINO

Hey, man, I'm not –

DUDE

Who're you working for? Lebowski? Jackie Treehorn?

DA FINO

The Knutsons.

DUDE

The? Who the fff–

DA FINO

The Knutsons. It's a wandering daughter job. Bunny

Lebowski, man. Her real name is Fawn Knutson. Her parents want her back.

He is fumbling in his wallet.

... See?

The Dude looks at the picture.

It is probably a school portrait, unmistakably Bunny, but fresh-faced, younger-looking, with a corn-fed smile and straight-banged Partridge Family *hair.*

> DUDE
> Jesus fucking Christ.

> DA FINO
> Crazy, huh? Ran away a year ago . . .

He is holding out another picture.

... The Knutsons told me to show her this when I found her. The family farm . . .

A bleak farmhouse and silo are the only features on a flat snow-swept landscape.

... outside of Moorhead, Minnesota. They think it'll make her homesick.

> DUDE
> Boy. How ya gonna keep 'em down on the farm once they seen Karl Hungus.

He hands back the picture.

... She's been kidnapped, Da Fino. Or maybe not, but she's definitely not around.

> DA FINO
> Fuck, man! That's terrible!

> DUDE
> Yeah, it sucks.

DA FINO

Well maybe you and me could pool our resources – trade
information – professional courtesy – compeers, you
know –

*We hear distant yapping, growing louder with the hum of an
approaching car.*

DUDE

Yeah, I get it. Fuck off, Da Fino. And stay away from my
special la – from my fucking lady friend.

*The Dude steps out to meet Walter's car, which pulls up with the
yapping Pomeranian leaning out of its open passenger window.*

DENNY'S

*Four scowling people sit at a booth: Uli, Kieffer, Franz and a young
woman with long stringy blond hair, dressed in patched jeans and a
ribbed sleeveless undershirt worn thin with age. She is apparently
bra-less and is Teutonically pale, with birthmarks on her face and arms.*

*Notable is her camera-side leg, which ends in a bandage-swaddled
foot. Dried rust-colored blood stains the tip of the bandage.*

The four are arguing, loudly, in German.

A waitress enters with an order pad.

WAITRESS

You folks ready?

The German shouting stops. Uli looks up sourly.

ULI

I haff lingenberry pancakes.

KIEFFER

Lingenberry pancakes.

FRANZ

Sree picks in blanket.

*The pale woman speaks to Uli in German. He relays a translation to
the waitress:*

116

ULI

Lingenberry pancakes.

WALTER'S CAR

Walter's eyes are on the road as he listens, driving, to the Dude, whose speech is occasionally punctuated by yaps from the back seat.

DUDE

I mean we totally fucked it up, man. We fucked up his pay-off, and got the kidnappers all pissed off, and the Big Lebowski yelled at me a lot, but he didn't *do* anything. Huh?

WALTER

Well it's, sometimes the cathartic, uh . . .

DUDE

I'm saying if he knows I'm a fuck-up, then why does he still leave me in charge of getting back his wife? Because he fucking doesn't *want* her back, man! He's had enough! He no longer digs her! It's all a show! But then, why didn't he give a shit about his million bucks? I mean, he knew we didn't hand off his briefcase, but he *never asked for it back.*

WALTER

What's your point, Dude?

DUDE

His million bucks was never *in* it, man! There was no money in that briefcase! He was *hoping* they'd kill her! You threw out a ringer for a ringer!

WALTER

Yeah?

DUDE

Shit yeah!

WALTER

Okay, but how does all this add up to an emergency?

DUDE

. . . Huh?

117

WALTER

I'm saying, I see what you're getting at, Dude. He kept the
money, but *my* point is, here we are, it's shabbas, the
sabbath, which I'm allowed to break only if it's a matter of
life or death –

DUDE

Walter, come off it. You're not even fucking Jewish, you're –

WALTER

What the fuck are you talking about?

DUDE

You're fucking Polish Catholic –

WALTER

What the fuck are you talking about? I converted when I
married Cynthia! Come on, Dude!

DUDE

Yeah, and you were –

WALTER

You know this!

DUDE

And you were divorced five fucking years ago.

WALTER

Yeah? What do you think happens when you get divorced?
You turn in your library card? Get a new driver's license?
Stop being Jewish?

DUDE

This driveway.

As he turns into the driveway:

WALTER

I'm as Jewish as fucking Tevye –

DUDE

It's just part of your whole sick Cynthia thing. Taking care
of her fucking dog. Going to her fucking synagogue. You're
living in the fucking past.

118

WALTER

Three thousand years of beautiful tradition, from Moses to
Sandy Koufax – YOU'RE GODDAMN RIGHT I LIVE IN THE PAST!
I – Jesus . . . What the hell happened?

He is looking off as the car slows. The Dude follows his look.

THE LEBOWSKI MANSION

*Walter's car pulls up the drive into the foreground and he and the
Dude emerge.*

Both are looking off at the front lawn.

WALTER

. . . Jesus Christ.

*Tire treads lead across the manicured lawn to where a little red sports
car rests with its hood crumpled into a palm trunk.*

TRACKING DOWN THE GREAT HALLWAY

*Through the French doors at its far end we can see Bunny, naked,
briefly bouncing on a diving board before splashing into the
illuminated pool outside.*

*Brandt, approaching, stoops and straightens, stoops and straightens,
picking up the discarded clothes that run the length of the hallway.*

BRANDT

He can't see you, Dude.

*The Dude and Walter nevertheless continue toward the study. Walter's
dog follows, stiffly wagging its tail.*

DUDE

Where'd she been?

BRANDT

Visiting friends of hers in Palm Springs. Just picked up and
left, never bothered to tell us.

DUDE

But I guess she told Uli.

WALTER

Jesus, Dude! She never even kidnapped her*self*!

BRANDT

Who's this gentleman, Dude?

WALTER

Who'm *I*? I'm a fucking VETERAN!

BRANDT

You shouldn't go in there, Dude! He's very angry!

BANG – the Dude and Walter push through the double doors into –

THE GREAT ROOM

The Big Lebowski turns at the sound of the door, his wheelchair humming as it spins.

LEBOWSKI
(bitterly)

Well, she's back. No thanks to you.

DUDE

Where's the money, Lebowski?

WALTER

A MILLION BUCKS FROM FUCKING NEEDY LITTLE URBAN ACHIEVERS! YOU ARE SCUM, MAN!

LEBOWSKI

Who the hell is he?

WALTER

I'll tell you who I am! I'm the guy who's gonna KICK YOUR PHONY GOLDBRICKING ASS!

DUDE

We know the briefcase was empty, man. We know you kept the million bucks yourself.

LEBOWSKI

Well, you have your story, I have mine. I say I entrusted the money to you, and you stole it.

WALTER

AS IF WE WOULD EVER *DREAM* OF TAKING YOUR BULLSHIT MONEY!

DUDE

You thought Bunny'd been kidnapped and you could use it as a pretext to make some money disappear. All you needed was a sap to pin it on, and you'd just met me, you human paraquat! You thought, hey, a deadbeat, a loser, someone the square community won't give a shit about!

LEBOWSKI

Well? Aren't you?

DUDE

Well . . . yeah . . .

LEBOWSKI

All right, get out. Both of you.

WALTER

Look at that fucking phony, Dude! Pretending to be a fucking millionaire!

LEBOWSKI

I said out. Now.

WALTER

Let me tell you something else. I've seen a lot of spinals, Dude, and this guy is a fake. A fucking goldbricker . . .

He is advancing on Lebowski.

. . . This guy fucking walks. I've never been more certain of anything in my life!

LEBOWSKI

Stay away from me, mister!

Walter hoists the Big Lebowski out of his wheelchair by the armpits.

WALTER

Walk, you fucking phony!

The Big Lebowski waggles helplessly, his rubbery feet grazing the floor like a Raggedy Ann's. The Pomeranian gaily leaps and yaps.

Upsy-daisy!

LEBOWSKI
Put me down, you son of a bitch!

DUDE
Walter!

WALTER
It's all over, man! We call your fucking bluff!

DUDE
WALTER, FOR CHRIST'S SAKE! HE'S CRIPPLED! PUT HIM DOWN!

WALTER
Sure, I'll put him down, Dude. RAUS! ACHTUNG, BABY!

He shoves the Big Lebowski forward and – Lebowski crumples to the floor, weeping.

WALTER
. . . Oh, shit.

LEBOWSKI
You're bullies! Cowards, both of you!

The Big Lebowski flails about on the floor. Walter is abashed.

WALTER
. . . Oh, shit.

DUDE
He can't walk, Walter!

WALTER
Yeah, I can see that, Dude.

LEBOWSKI
You monsters!

DUDE
Help me put him back in his chair.

WALTER
Shit, sorry man.

LEBOWSKI
(through his tears)
Stay away from me! You bullies! You and these women! You
won't leave a man his fucking balls!

DUDE
Walter, you fuck!

WALTER
Shit, Dude, I didn't know. I wouldn't've done it if I knew
he was a fucking crybaby.

DUDE
We're sorry, man. We're really sorry.

*Having gotten him into his chair, the Dude picks up the Big Lebowski's
plaid lap warmer and frantically tucks it back in around his waist,
meanwhile batting away the dog.*

. . . There ya go. Sorry man . . .

Walter, puzzled, hands on hips, stands over the Big Lebowski.

WALTER
Shit. He didn't *look* like a spinal.

TEN PINS

Scattered at the cut.

*The Dude and Walter sit with beers at the scoring table as Donny
enters.*

WALTER
Sure you'll see some tank battles. But fighting in desert is
very different from fighting in canopy jungle.

DUDE
Uh-huh.

WALTER

I mean 'Nam was a foot soldier's war whereas, uh, this thing should be a fucking cakewalk. I mean I had an M16, Jacko, not an Abrams fucking tank. Just me and Charlie, man. Eyeball to eyeball.

DUDE

Yeah.

WALTER

That's fuckin' combat. The man in the black pyjamas, Dude. Worthy fuckin' adversary.

DONNY

Who's in pyjamas, Walter?

WALTER

Shut the fuck up, Donny. Not a bunch of fig-eaters with towels on their heads tryin' to find reverse on a Soviet tank. This is not a worthy –

VOICE

HEY!

Quintana, bellowing from the lip of the lane, is restrained by O'Brien.

QUINTANA

. . . What's this 'day of rest' shit, man?!

Walter looks at him innocently.

. . . What is this bullshit, man? I don't fucking care! It don't matter to Jesus! But you're not fooling me! You might fool the fucks in the league office, but you don't fool Jesus! It's bush league psych-out stuff! Laughable, man! I would've fucked you in the ass Saturday, I'll fuck you in the ass next Wednesday instead!

He makes hip-grinding coital motions as O'Brien leads him away.

. . . You got a date Wednesday, man!

Walter, his head cocked, and the Dude, peeking over his shades, watch him go.

WALTER

... He's cracking.

BOWLING ALLEY PARKING LOT

Donny, Walter and the Dude emerge from the alley, each holding his leatherette ball satchel.

WALTER

– the whole concept of aish. That's why, in the fourteenth century, the Rambam said . . .

His voice trails off as he reacts to the droning synthesizer-based techno-pop coming from a boom box.

Uli, Kieffer and Franz, in shiny black leather, stand in a line facing the three bowlers in the deserted lot. Behind them orange flames lick gently at the Dude's car, which has been put to the torch. The reflected flames glow on the men's creaking leather.

Next to the car are three motorcycles, parked neatly in a row.

The Dude looks sadly at his burning car.

DUDE

They finally did it. They killed my fucking car.

ULI

Vee vant zat money, Lebowski.

KIEFFER

Ja, uzzervize vee killseckurl.

FRANZ

Ja, it seems you forgot our little deal, Lebowski.

DUDE

You don't *have* the fucking girl, dipshits. We know you never did. So you've got nothing on my Johnson.

The men in black, stunned, confer amongst themselves.

DONNY
(*under his breath*)

Are these the Nazis, Walter?

Walter answers, also sotto voce, *his eyes still on the three men:*

WALTER

They're nihilists, Donny, nothing to be afraid of.

The Germans stop conferring.

ULI

Vee don't care. Vee still vant zat money or vee fuck you upp.

KIEFFER

Ja, vee still fontsa money. Vee sreaten you.

He pulls an Uzi from under his coat. It glints in the firelight.

WALTER

Fuck you. Fuck the three of you.

DUDE

Hey, cool it, Walter.

WALTER

There's no ransom if you don't have a fucking hostage!
That's what ransom *is*. Those are the fucking *rules*.

ULI

Zere ARE no ROOLZ!

WALTER

NO RULES?! WHY YOU CABBAGE-EATING SONS-OF-BITCHES –

KIEFFER

His girlfriend gafe up her toe! She sought we'd be getting
million dollars! Iss not fair!

WALTER

Fair! WHO'S THE FUCKING NIHILIST HERE! WHAT ARE YOU, A
BUNCH OF FUCKING CRYBABIES?!

DUDE

Hey, cool it, Walter. Listen, pal, there never was any money.
The Big Lebowski gave me an empty briefcase, man, so
take it up with him.

WALTER

AND I'D LIKE MY UNDIES BACK!

The Germans again confer amongst themselves.

Donny is frightened.

> DONNY
>
> Are they gonna hurt us, Walter?

Walter's tone is gentle:

> WALTER
>
> They won't hurt us, Donny. These men are cowards.

> ULI
>
> Okay. Vee take ze money you haf on you und vee call sit eefen.

> WALTER
>
> Fuck you.

The Dude is digging into his pocket:

> DUDE
>
> Come on, Walter, we're ending this thing cheap.

> WALTER
>
> What's mine is mine.

> DUDE
>
> Come on, Walter!
> *(louder, to the Germans, as he looks in his wallet)*
> . . . Four dollars here!

He inspects the change in his palm:

> . . . Almost five!

> DONNY
> *(tremulously)*
> I got eighteen dollars, Dude.

> WALTER
> *(grimly)*
> What's mine is mine.

With a ring of steel, Uli produces a glinting saber.

> ULI
>
> VEE FUCK YOU UPP, MAN! VEE TAKE YOUR MONEY!

                    WALTER
                    (*coolly*)
Come and get it.

                       ULI
VEE FUCK YOU UPP, MAN!

                    WALTER
Come and get it. Fucking nihilist.

                       ULI
I FUCK YOU! I FUCK YOU!

                    WALTER
Show me what you got. Nihilist. Dipshit with a nine-toed
woman.

Goaded into rage, Uli charges:

                       ULI
I FUCK YOU! I FUCK YOU!

Walter hurls his leather satchel.

*Kieffer, watching Uli's charge, is caught off-guard. The bowling ball
thuds into his chest and lifts him off his feet.*

He falls back, his Uzi clattering away.

*Walter twists away as Uli reaches him and grabs Uli's head in both
hands. He draws Uli's head up to his mouth and locks onto his ear.*

*The Dude rushes Franz but draws up short as Franz sends out karate
kicks, his leather pants squeaking and popping. Franz givesa loud
cry with each kick; the Dude leans back, throwing his arms up,
evading the kicks.*

*Walter's jaw is still clamped on Uli's ear as Uli draws his saber
against Walter's side, drawing blood.*

*Walter doesn't react to the wound. He worries the ear, growling, his
jaw clamped and his head waggling.*

Uli drops the saber.

                       130

The Dude awkwardly circles Franz, evading his kicks.

Walter continues to worry the ear until, with a tearing sound, his head and Uli's separate.

Uli, earless, screams:

> ULI
> I FUCK YOU! YOU CANNOT HURT ME! I BELIEF IN NUSSING!

Walter spits his ear into his face.

The Dude and Franz, both now panting heavily, have yet to establish body contact. Franz continues to kick.

> FRANZ
> VEAKLING!

Walter draws his fist back as Uli bellows:

> ULI
> NUSSING!

> WALTER
> ANTI-SEMITE!

BAM! – A powerhouse blow to the middle of his face drops Uli for the count.

With a piercing shriek, Franz finally summons the nerve to charge the Dude, hands tensed to deliver karate blows.

As he reaches the Dude – WHHAP – the boom box swings into frame to smash him in the face. Its volume shoots up.

Walter bashes him a few more times over the head. The music screeches to static, then quiet.

All quiet.

Walter, panting, looks around.

> WALTER
> We've got a man down, Dude.

With a hand pressed to his bleeding side he trots over to Donny, who lies gasping on the ground.

The Dude, panting as well, also trots over.

> DUDE
>
> My God! They shot him, Walter!

> WALTER
>
> No Dude.

> DUDE
>
> They shot Donny!

Donny gasps for air. His eyes, wide, go from the Dude to Walter. One hand still clutches his eighteen dollars.

> WALTER
>
> There weren't any shots.

> DUDE
>
> Then what's –

> WALTER
>
> It's a heart attack.

> DUDE
>
> Wha . . .

> WALTER
>
> Call the medics, Dude.

> DUDE
>
> Wha . . . Donny –

> WALTER
>
> Hurry, Dude. I'd go but I'm pumping blood. Might pass out.

The Dude runs into the lanes.

Walter lays a reassuring hand on Donny's shoulder.

> . . . Rest easy, good buddy, you're doing fine. We got help choppering in.

FADE OUT

HOLD IN BLACK

THE DUDE AND WALTER

They sit side by side, forearms on knees, in a nondescript waiting area.
Walter bounces the fingertips of one hand off those of the other. They
sit. They wait.

A tall thin man in a conservative black suit enters. He takes in the
Dude's bowling attire and sunglasses and Walter's army surplus, but
doesn't make an issue of it.

MAN

Hello, gentlemen. You are the bereaved?

DUDE

Yeah man.

MAN

Francis Donnelly. Pleased to meet you.

DUDE

Jeffrey Lebowski.

WALTER

Walter Sobchak.

DUDE

The Dude, actually. Is what, uh . . .

DONNELLY

Excuse me?

DUDE

Nothing.

DONNELLY

Yes. I understand you're taking away the remains.

WALTER

Yeah.

DONNELLY

We have the urn . . .

He nods toward a door.

. . . And I assume this is credit card?

He is vaguely handing a large leather folder across the desk to whomever wants to take it.

WALTER

Yeah.

He accepts it, opens it, puts on reading glasses that sit halfway down his nose, and inspects the bill with his head pulled back for focus and cocked for concentration.

Silence.

The Dude smiles at Donnelly.

Donnelly gives back a mortician's smile.

134

At length Walter holds the bill toward Donnelly, pointing.

... What's this?

DONNELLY

That is for the urn.

WALTER

Don't need it. We're scattering the ashes.

DONNELLY

Yes, so we were informed. However, we must of course transmit the remains to you in a receptacle.

WALTER

This is a hundred and eighty dollars.

DONNELLY

Yes, sir. It is our most modestly priced receptacle.

DUDE

Well can we –

WALTER

A hundred and eighty dollars?!

DONNELLY

They range up to three thousand.

WALTER

Yeah, but we're –

DUDE

Can we just rent it from you?

DONNELLY

Sir, this is a mortuary, not a rental house.

WALTER

We're scattering the fucking ashes!

DUDE

Walter –

WALTER

JUST BECAUSE WE'RE BEREAVED DOESN'T MEAN WE'RE SAPS!

Sir, please lower your voice –

Hey man, don't you have something else you could put it in?

That is our most modestly priced receptacle.

GODDAMNIT! IS THERE A RALPH'S AROUND HERE?!

POINT DUME

It is a high, wind-swept bluff. Walter and the Dude approach its edge. Walter is carrying a bright-red coffee can with a blue plastic lid.

When they reach the edge the two men stand awkwardly for a beat. Finally:

. . . I'll say a few words.

The Dude clasps his hands in front of him. Walter clears his throat.

. . . Donny was a good bowler, and a good man. He was . . . He was one of us. He was a man who loved the outdoors, and bowling, and as a surfer explored the beaches of southern California from Redondo to Calabassos. And he was an avid bowler. And a good friend. He died – he died as so many of his generation, before his time. In your wisdom you took him, Lord. As you took so many bright flowering young men, at Khe San and Lan Doc and Hill 364. These young men gave their lives. And Donny too. Donny who . . . who loved bowling . . .

Walter clears his throat.

. . . And so, Theodore – Donald – Karabotsos, in accordance with what we think your dying wishes might well have been, we commit your mortal remains to the bosom of . . .

Walter is peeling the lid off the coffee can.

... the Pacific Ocean, which you loved so well ...

As he shakes out the ashes.

... Goodnight, sweet prince ...

The wind blows all of the ashes into the Dude, standing just to the side of and behind Walter.

The Dude stands, frozen.

His eulogy complete, Walter looks back.

... Shit, I'm sorry Dude.

He starts brushing off the Dude with his hands.

... Goddamn wind.

Heretofore motionless, the Dude now explodes, slapping Walter's hands away.

DUDE
Goddamnit, Walter! You fucking asshole!

WALTER
Dude! Dude, I'm sorry!

DUDE

You make everything a fucking travesty!

WALTER

Dude, I'm – It was an accident!

The Dude gives Walter a furious shove.

DUDE

What about that shit about Vietnam!

WALTER

Dude, I'm sorry –

DUDE

What the fuck does Vietnam have to do with anything! What
the fuck were you talking about?!

Walter, for the first time, is genuinely distressed, almost lost.

WALTER

Shit, Dude, I'm sorry –

DUDE

You're a fuck, Walter!

*He gives Walter a weaker shove. Walter seems dazed, then wraps his
arms around the Dude.*

WALTER

Awww, fuck it, Dude. Let's go bowling.

BOWLING ALLEY BAR

The Dude walks up.

DUDE

Two oat sodas, Gary.

GARY

Right. Good luck tomorrow.

DUDE

Thanks, man.

GARY

Sorry to hear about Donny.

DUDE

Yeah. Well, you know, sometimes you eat the bear, and, uh . . .

'Tumbling Tumbleweeds' has come up on the jukebox, and The Stranger ambles up to the bar.

THE STRANGER

Howdy do, Dude.

DUDE

Oh, hey man, how are ya? I wondered if I'd see you again.

THE STRANGER

Wouldn't miss the semis. How things been goin'?

DUDE

Ahh, you know. Strikes and gutters, ups and downs.

The Stranger's eyes crinkle merrily.

THE STRANGER

Sure, I gotcha.

The bartender puts two gleaming beers on the bar.

DUDE

Thanks, Gary . . . Take care, man, I gotta get back.

THE STRANGER

Sure. Take it easy, Dude – I know that you will.

The Dude, leaving, nods.

DUDE

Yeah man. Well, you know, the Dude abides.

Gazing after him, The Stranger drawls, savoring the words:

THE STRANGER

The Dude abides . . .

As his head shakes appreciation, his eyes find the camera.

... I don't know about you, but I take comfort in that. It's good knowin' he's out there, the Dude, takin' her easy for all us sinners. Shoosh. I sure hope he makes the finals. Welp, that about does her, wraps her all up. Things seem to've worked out pretty good for the Dude 'n' Walter, and it was a purt good story, dontcha think? Made me laugh to beat the band. Parts, anyway. Course – I didn't like seein' Donny go. But then, I happen to know that there's a little Lebowski on the way. I guess that's the way the whole durned human comedy keeps perpetuatin' itself, down through the generations, westward the wagons, across the sands a time until – aw, look at me, I'm ramblin' again. Wal, uh hope you folks enjoyed yourselves ...

He brushes his hat brim with a fingertip as we begin to pull back.

... Catch ya further on down the trail.

As we pull away The Stranger swivels in to the bar, and his voice fades:

... Say, friend, ya got any more a that good sarsaparilla? ...

CREDITS

POLYGRAM FILMED ENTERTAINMENT PRESENTS
A WORKING TITLE PRODUCTION

THE BIG LEBOWSKI

Casting	by John Lyons, CSA
Supervising Sound Editor	Skip Lievsay
Edited by	Roderick Jaynes and Tricia Cooke
Original Music by	Carter Burwell
Musical Archivist	T-Bone Burnett
Costume Designer	Mary Zophres
Production Designer	Rick Heinrichs
Director of Photography	Roger Deakins ASC, BSC
Co-Producer	John Cameron
Executive Producers	Tim Bevan and Eric Fellner
Produced by	Ethan Coen
Written by	Ethan Coen and Joel Coen
Directed by	Joel Coen

CAST

THE DUDE	Jeff Bridges
WALTER SOBCHAK	John Goodman
MAUDE LEBOWSKI	Julianne Moore
DONNY	Steve Buscemi
THE BIG LEBOWSKI	David Huddleston
BRANDT	Philip Seymour Hoffman
BUNNY LEBOWSKI	Tara Reid
TREEHORN THUGS	Philip Moon, Mark Pellegrino
NIHILISTS	Peter Stormare, Flea, Torsten Voges
SMOKEY	Jimmie Dale Gilmore
DUDE'S LANDLORD	Jack Kehler
JESUS QUINTANA	John Turturro
QUINTANA'S PARTNER	James G. Hoosier
MAUDE'S THUGS	Carlos Leon, Terrance Burton
OLDER COP	Richard Gant
YOUNGER COP	Christian Clemenson

TONY THE CHAUFFEUR	Dom Irrera
LEBOWSKI'S CHAUFFEUR	Gerard L'Heureux
KNOX HARRINGTON	David Thewlis
COFFEE SHOP WAITRESS	Lu Elrod
AUTO CIRCUS COP	Michael Gomez
GARY THE BARTENDER	Peter Siragusa
THE STRANGER	Sam Elliott
DOCTOR	Marshall Manesh
ARTHUR DIGBY SELLERS	Harry Bugin
LITTLE LARRY SELLERS	Jesse Flanagan
PILAR	Irene Olga Lopez
CORVETTE OWNER	Luis Colina
JACKIE TREEHORN	Ben Gazzara
MALIBU POLICE CHIEF	Leon Russom
CAB DRIVER	Ajgie Kirkland
PRIVATE SNOOP	Jon Polito
NIHILIST WOMAN	Aimee Mann
SADDAM	Jerry Haleva
PANCAKE WAITRESS	Jennifer Lamb
FUNERAL DIRECTOR	Warren David Keith
STUNT COORDINATOR	Jery Hewitt
STUNTS	Jennifer Lamb, Vince Deadrick Jr., Loyd Catlett

CREW

Unit Production Manager	John Cameron
First Assistant Director	Jeff Rafner
Key Second Assistant Director	Conte Mark Matal
Production Supervisor	Gilly Ruben
Accountant	Mindy Sheldon
Visual Effects Supervisor	Janek Sirrs
Choreographers	Bill and Jacqui Landarum
Art Director	John Dexter
Set Decorator	Chris Spellman
Location Manager	Robert Graf
Assistant Location Manager	Kim Jordan
Camera Operator	Ted Morris
First Assistant Camera	Andy Harris
Second Assistant Camera	Adam Gilmore
Camera Loader	Ed Dally
Still Photograher	Merrick Morton
Chief Lighting Technician	Bill O'Leary

Assistant Chief Lighting Technicians	Alan P. Colbert, Alan Frazier
Electricians	Roman Jakobi, Jon Salzman, Duncan M. Sobel, Abbe Wool
Rigging Gaffer	Marty Bosworth
Rigging Best Boy Electric	Chris Reddish
Rigging Electricians	Craig A. Brink, David Diamond, Jimmy Ellis, Jenifer Galvez, Kevin Brown
First Company Grip	Les Percy
Second Company Grip	Wayne Kosky
Dolly Grip	Bruce Hamme
Grips	Charlie Edwards, Tony Boura, Charles Smith
Key Rigging Grip	Jerry Day
Rigging Best Boy Grip	Bill Green
Rigging Grips	Alvaro Martinez, Phil Aubry, Michael Stringer, Robert King
Sound Mixer	Allan Byer
Boom Operators	Keenan Wyatt, Peter Kurland
Utility Sound Technician	Sam Sarkar
Script Supervisor	T. Kukowinski
Second Second Assistant Director	Donald Murphy
Production Coordinator	Gregg Edler
Assistant Production Coordinator	Tom Elkins
Production Secretary	Kimberly Rach
Big Associate Editor	Big Dave Diliberto
Assistant Editors	Lisa Mozden, Alex Belth
Apprentice Editor	Karyn Anonia
Dialogue Editors	Magdaline Volaitis, Rick Freeman
ADR Editor	Kenton Jakub
FX Editor	Lewis Goldstein
Foley Mixer	Bruce Pross
Foley Artist	Marko Costanzo
Foley Editors	Jennifer Ralston, Frank Kern
Assistant Sound Editors	Kimberly McCord, Wyatt Sprague
Transfer Assistant Editor	Anne Pope
Foley Supervisor	Ben Cheah
Apprentice Sound Editor	Allan Zaleski
Intern Sound Editor	Igor Nicholich
Dolby Consultant	Bradford Hohle
Re-Recording Mixers	Michael Barry, Skip Lievsay
Music Editor	Todd Kasow

Associate Music Editor	Missy Cohen
Executive in Charge of Production	Jane Frazer
Storyboard Artist	J. Todd Anderson
Set Designer	Mariko Braswell
Graphic Designer	Bradford Richardson
Art Department Coordinator	Lori Ashcraft
Leadperson	Tim Snowber
Co-Leadperson	Karen Agresti
On-Set Dresser	Lisa A. Corbin
Set Dressers	Beth Emerson, Tim Park
Property Master	Ritchie Kremer
Assistant Property Master	Ron Patterson
Property Handler	Carolyn Lassek
Make-up Supervisor	Jean Black
Make-up for Mr. Bridges	Edouard Henriques
Hair Stylist	Daniel Curet
Assistant Costume Designer	Sonya Ooten
Costume Supervisor	Pam Withers
Key Set Costumer	Cookie Lopez
Set Costumer	Virginia Seffens-Burton
Visual Effects by	The Computer Film Company, Inc.
Visual Effects Producer	Janet Yale
Compositing Artists	David Fuhrer, Travis Bauman, Donovan Scott
3D Artist	Robert Chapin
Paint Artists	Katie Hecker, Susan Evans, Matt Dessero
Mechanical Effects Designer	Peter Chesney
Special Effects Foremen	Tom Chesney, Mick Duff
Effects Technicians	Chris Nelson, Barry Beaulac
Assistant Accountant	Kris Soderquist
Payroll Accountant	Jery Legget
Accounting Production Assistant	Aillene Laure Bubis
Post Production Supervisor	Charlie Vogel
Casting Associate	Wendy Weidman
Casting Assistant	Jenna Dupree
Extras Casting Coordinator	Cecily Jordan
Extras Casting Assistant	Fonda Anita
Aerial Cameraman	Ron Goodman
Aerial Camera Assistants	Dave Sale, Jeremy Braben
Music Playback	Brian McCarty
Video Assist	Marty Weight

Publicist	Larry Kaplan
Dialect Coach	Liz Himelstein
Bowling Pro	Barry Asher
First Aid	Thomas W. Foster, Jonas C. Matz
Construction Coordinator	Tim Lafferty
Construction Estimator	Kathleen Walker
Propmaker Foremen	David Boucher, Franklin P. Healy
Propmaker Gang Bosses	Douglas Dewaay, Mark Haber, Aaron Harney, Brett Hernandez, Steven D. Powell
Laborer Foreman	Charles Reyes
Laborer Gang Boss	Philip Vargas
Tool Man	Larry Wise
Head Painter	Anthony Gaudio
Stand-by Painter	John Railton
Painter Foremen	Wayne Nycz, Gary Osborn
Greensman	Philip C. Hurst
Transportation Coordinator	Don Tardino
Transportation Captains	Thomas Vilardo, Tim Ryan
Transportation Estimator	Derek Wade
Production Van Drivers	Michael E. Cain, Anthony K. Riedel
Honeywagon Driver	Dennis Junt
Office Assistant	Marty Houston
Set Production Assistants	Rita Lisa Danao, Randol P. Taylor, Tammy Dickson
Company Coordinator	Nina Khoshaba
Location Assistants	Chris Fuentes, Valerie Jo Burnley
Art Department Assistant	Sydney Ann Lunn
Assistant to Mr. Goodman	Particia Douglas
Assistant to Mr. Bevan	Juliette Dow
Assistants to Mr. Fellner	Amelia Granger, Lara Thompson
Production Goddess	Karyn Anonia
Production Interns	Stacy Minkowsky, Lauren Lapham
Stand-Ins	Ken Kells, Frank Turner
Catering	Entertainment Motion Picture Catering, Clement Bacque, Eric Vignando
Crafts Service	Gary Kramer
Baby Wranglers	Patti Cooke, Eileen Sullivan
Giggles/Howls/Marmots	William Preston Robertson
Animals	Animal Actors

Left Behind	Margaret Hayes
President of Operations for Mike Zoss Productions	Alan J. Schoolcraft

Animal action was monitored by the
AMERICAN HUMANE ASSOCIATION
Scenes which appear to place an animal in jeopardy were simulated.
No animal was harmed during the making of this film.

Special Thanks

CLAY RAND

CINEMA VEHICLE SERVICES

HOLLYWOOD STAR LANES

AMSPEC

BRIAN BILES

EMIL MOSCOWITZ

PATRICK SHEEDY

GARY SPERO

LIZ YOUNG

SEÑOR GREASER

Legal Services	Shays & Murphy
Financial Consultant	Rashid Chinchanwala
Legal Advisors	Angela Morrison, Rachel Holroyd
Post Production Facilities	C5, Sound One Corporation
Opticals by	John Alagna, The Effects House, Janos Pilenyi, Cineric Inc.
Negative Cutter	Mo Henry
Color Timer	David Orr

Title Sequence and 'Gutterballs' Titles
Designed and Produced by
BALSMEYER & EVERETT, INC.

Designer	Randall Balsmeyer
Animation Producer	Kathy Kelehan
Computer Animators	Daniel Leung, Amit Sethi, Matt McDonald, Gray Miller

Dancers

Holly Copeland	Karen Christenberry	Natalie Webb
Julie Bond	Kim Yates	Elizabeth A. Eaton
Lori Jo Birdsell	Kelly Sheerin	Kiva Dawson
Lisa C. Boltauzer	Alison Simpson	Lindsay Fellenbaum
Melissa Aggeles	Katherine Slay	Jennifer S. Garett

146

Danielle Nicole Parish	Jennifer Strovas	Jamie Green
Caitlin McLean	Michelle E. Swanson	Laurel Kitten
Joelle Martinec	Amy Tinkham	Mary Lee
Sandra Plazinic	Bree Turner	Carrie Macy
Jacqui Landrum	Martina Volpp	Danielle Marcus Janssen
Wendy Braun	Amy Warren	Michelle Rudy-Mirkovich

Original Music Orchestrated by	Carter Burwell, Sonny Kompanek
Music Engineer	Michael Farrow
Music Contractor	Emile Charlap
Recorded at	Right Track Recording, New York City
Music Supervisor	Happy Walters
Executive in Charge of Music for PolyGram Filmed Entertainment	Dawn Solér
Senior VP for PolyGram Soundtracks	Jacquie Perrymnan
Music Coordinators	Spring Aspers, Manish Raval, Tom Wolfe

'THE MAN IN ME'
Written and Performed by Bob Dylan
Published by Big Sky Music (SESAC)
Courtesy of Columbia Records
By arrangement with Sony Music
Licensing

'ATAYPURA'
Written by Moises Vivanco
Performed by Yma Sumac
Published by Beechwood Music Corp.
(BMI)
Courtesy of Capitol Records
Under License from EMI-Capitol
Music Special Markets

'BEHAVE YOURSELF'
Written by Booker T. Jones, Steve
Cropper, Al Jackson Jr. and Lewie
Steinberg
Performed by Booker T. & The MGs
Published by Irving Music, Inc. (BMI)
Courtesy of Atlantic Recording Corp.
By arrangement with Warner Special
Products

'BRANDED' Theme song
Written by Alan Alch and Dominic
Frontiere
Published by EMI Unart Catalog Inc.
(BMI)

'DEAD FLOWERS'
Written by Mick Jagger and Keith
Richards
Published by Abkco Music, Inc.
Performed by Townes Van Zandt
Courtesy of Sugar Hill Records

'GLÜCK DAS MIR VERBLIEB'
from the opera 'DIE TOTE STADT'
Written and conducted by Erich
Wolfgang Korngold
Performed by Ilona Steingruber, Anton
Dermota and the Austrian State Radio
Orchestra
Used by permission of European
American Music Distributors
Corporation, agent for Schott Musik
International
Courtesy of Cambria Master
Recordings

'HER EYES ARE A BLUE MILLION MILES'
Written by Don Vliet
Performed by Captain Beefheart
Published by EMI Unart Catalog Inc.
(BMI)
Courtesy of Reprise Records
By arrangement with Warner Special
Products

'HOTEL CALIFORNIA'
Written by Don Henley, Glenn Frey
and Don Felder
Performed by The Gipsy Kings
Published by Cass County Music
(BMI)/Red Cloud Music (BMI)/
Fingers Music (ASCAP)
Courtesy of Elektra Entertainment
Group
By arrangement with Warner Special
Products and Pem/Sine (Sony Music
Independent Network Europe)

'I GOT IT BAD & THAT AIN'T GOOD'
Written by Duke Ellington and Paul
Francis Webster
Performed by Nina Simone
Published by Webster Music Co./EMI
Robbins Catalog, Inc. (ASCAP)
Courtesy of Rhino Records
By arrangement with Warner Special
Products
Nina Simone appears by special
arrangement with Nina Simone and
Steven Ames Brown

'I HATE YOU'
Written by Gary Burger, David
Havlicek, Roger Johnston, Thomas E.
Shaw and Larry Spangler
Performed by Monks
Published by Monktime Publishing
(BMI)/Administererd by Bug
Courtesy of Polydor GMBH, Hamburg
By arrangement with PolyGram Film &
TV Music

'JUST DROPPED IN (TO SEE WHAT
CONDITION MY CONDITION WAS IN)'
Written by Mickey Newbury
Performed by Kenny Rogers & The
First Edition
Published by Acuff-Rose Music, Inc.
(BMI)
Courtesy of MCA Records
Under license from Universal Music
Special Markets

'LOOKIN' OUT MY BACK DOOR'
Written by John Fogerty
Performed by Creedence Clearwater
Revival
Published by Jondora Music (BMI)
Courtesy of Fantasy Inc.

'LUJON'
Written and Performed by Henry
Mancini
Published by Northridge Music,
Administered by MCA Music
Publishing, A division of Universal
Studios, Inc. (ASCAP)
Courtesy of the RCA Records Label of
BMG Entertainment

'MUCHA MUCHACHA'
Written by Juan Garcia Esquivel
Performed by Esquivel
Published by MCA-Duchess Music
Corporation (BMI)
Courtesy of the RCA Records Label of
BMG Entertainment

'MY MOOD SWINGS'
Written by Elvis Costello and Cait
O'Riordan
Performed by Elvis Costello
Published by Sideways Music,
Administered by Plangent Visions
Music (ASCAP)

'OYE COMO VA'
Written by Tito Puente
Performed by Santana
Published by Full Keel Music Co.
(ASCAP)
Courtesy of Columbia Records
By arrangement with Sony Music
Licensing

'PEACEFUL EASY FEELING'
Written by Jack Tempchin
Performed by The Eagles
Published by Jazz Bird Music/WB
Music Corp. (ASCAP)
Courtesy of Elektra Entertainment
Group
By arrangement with Warner Special
Products

'PIACERE SEQUENCE'
Written and Performed by Teo Usuelli
Published by West Edizioni Musicali
(SIAE)
Courtesy West Edizioni Musicali

'PICTURES AT AN EXHIBITION'
Written by Modest Moussorgsky
Performed by The Royal
Concertgebouw Orchestra
Conducted by Sir Colin Davis
Used by permission of Boosey &
Hawkes, Inc. (ASCAP)
Courtesy of Philips Classics
By arrangement with PolyGram Film &
TV Music

'REQUIEM IN D MINOR'
Written by W. A. Mozart
Performed by The Slovak
Philharmonic Orchestra and Choir
Published by Cezame Argile (ASCAP)
Courtesy of Audio Auction

'RUN THROUGH THE JUNGLE'
Written by John Fogerty
Performed by Creedence Clearwater
Revival
Published by Jondora Music (BMI)
Courtesy of Fantasy Inc.

'STAMPING GROUND'
Written by Louis Hardin (a.k.a.
Moondog)
Performed by Moondog with Orchestra
Published by Archimedes Music,
Administered for the world by Don
Williams Music Group, Inc. (ASCAP)
Courtesy of Sony Classical
By arrangement with Sony Music
Licensing

'STANDING ON THE CORNER'
Written by Frank Loesser
Performed by Dean Martin
Published by Frank Music Corp.
(ASCAP)
Courtesy of Capitol Records
Under license from EMI-Capitol
Music Special Markets

'TAMMY'
Written by Ray Evans and Jay
Livingston
Performed by Debbie Reynolds
Published by St Angelo Music,
Administered by MCA Music
Publishing, A division of Universal
Studios, Inc. (ASCAP)/Jay Livingston
Music, Inc. (ASCAP)
Courtesy of MCA Records
Under license from Universal Music
Special Markets

'TRAFFIC BOOM'
Written and Performed by Piero
Piccioni
Published by Edizioni Musicali Beat
Records Co. (SIAE)
Courtesy of Beat Records Co.